Maximizing Service Provider Relationships

Best Practices Through Blended Management

by
Maurice W. Scherrens

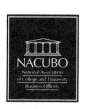

A NACUBO Publication

NACUBO would like to thank COLLEGIS
for its generous support in sponsoring this book.

ISBN 1-56972-008-8

Cover design by Andrea Richards

Senior Editor: Caroline M. Grills

Editor: Anne Kendrick

Designed and typeset by AAH Graphics, Fort Valley, Virginia

Printed and bound in the United States of America

ACKNOWLEDGMENTS

This is my first book, and what I have learned is that even this modest entry into authorship would not have been possible without the invaluable assistance and guidance from a number of friends and colleagues.

I am extremely grateful to Dr. George W. Johnson and Dr. Alan G. Merten, the two presidents of George Mason University (GMU) for whom I have had the great pleasure to serve during the past 20 years. They have given me not only the opportunity to help GMU become a national leader in the field of service outsourcing, but also the freedom to challenge the traditional systems of service delivery within higher education and develop new "best practice" prototypes, based on rigorous principles of continuous performance evaluation.

For their very helpful and thorough review of early drafts of the book, I would like to express my thanks to each of the NACUBO reviewers: Henry Rossi, Bryn Mawr; Nancy Eddy, Holyoke Community College; Ed Coate, Mira Costa Community College District; Bill Merck, University of Central Florida; and Elaine M. Watson, DePaul University, for providing their knowledge in the field of higher education business management. Additionally, it was both a professional and personal pleasure to work with the staff of NACUBO, particularly Caroline Grills, publications manager, and Donna Klinger, publications director, and Anne Kendrick, editor. For their professionalism and expertise, I am truly grateful.

I am deeply indebted to the administrative assistance provided by Jan Steele, Sharon Condia, and Kelly Mossey. The number of rewrites of this manuscript before it ever saw daylight outside the walls of GMU are too countless to contemplate. Thank you very much. The early technical research performed by Diane Turner, Marianne Serbu, and Heather Meyers was also invaluable. There would be no book had these three not completed the research and then kept me on an aggressive time schedule.

I am most appreciative of the time and effort contributed to this book by Barb Lubar and Benn Crandall, members of Educational Support Services (ESS) and part of the GMU family under partnership agreements for Events

Management and Auxiliary Enterprises. They often performed like my co-pilots. My navigator and my source of inspiration was Heather Meyers. Thanks. Friends and more forever.

Above all else, I dedicate this book to my parents who now reside in Holland, Michigan. From my earliest childhood memories, they instilled in me a "can-do" attitude, and a belief that there was no limit to what could be accomplished if you simply put your mind to it. I will be forever indebted to them for instilling in me a set of values and principles that have guided me through life. As the father of two wonderful daughters, Jessie and Genny, and one great son, Philip, I can only hope that I can pass on to them some of what my loving parents passed on to me. Their love is my daily inspiration.

CONTENTS

Part I
Agile Archers and Moving Targets

Part II
The Five-Step Unit Review Process and the High Five Approach to Blended Management

Part III
Lessons from the Journey

INTRODUCTION

"Life is a dance you learn as you go; sometimes you lead and sometimes you follow."

—John Michael Montgomery

Warning! This is a book about change, and about an institution's relentless drive to find and implement best practices for its support services. It is about the rigorous, often grueling self-assessment required to stay in step with the demands of our changing clientele. Some days it seems like we are making great strides toward our goals. On other days we feel like we have taken one step forward and two steps backward. This book is a compilation of support services theories, philosophies, and true life stories from George Mason University (GMU). We share them with you in spite of our awareness that what may have worked at GMU may simply not work within your particular organization. Some of our successes were affected by more variables than we could ever identify. Likewise some of our disappointments have been affected by a similar set of variables, peculiar to GMU at a given point in time in our history.

So our warning is simple: The lesson, if any, to be learned from our experiences lies in the process, not in the outcome.

The goal of this book is to demystify outsourcing, change and blended management, and to illustrate how you can successfully manage while embracing change. We think we have integrated change management into the fabric of our culture—so well, in fact, that before the print dries on any chapter in this book, we will have already readjusted our sights to focus on several new support service targets.

A key focus of this book is the development of outcome-oriented performance indicators and continuous self-assessment. We hope it will give you the tools you need to become a difference maker at your organization by showing others the importance of performance review. The book may also help you discover some strategies for building a culture not only comfortable with change, but uncomfortable without change.

The following quotes describe the culture that is being developed at George Mason University:

"Most ailing organizations have developed a functional blindness to their own defects. They are not suffering because they cannot resolve their problems, but because they cannot see their problems."

—John Gardner

"Everyday the world turns upside down on someone who thought they were sitting on top of it."

—Glen Tullman, President, CCC Information Services

Part I

Agile Archers and Moving Targets

In striving for best practices, many colleges and universities have long outsourced food and bookstore services. Today, institutions are broadening their reliance on outsourcing so that they can focus on their primary mission and doing what they do best. Outsourcing is a growing option that helps colleges and universities apply their internal resources toward core competencies. Organizations have increasingly come to depend on external partners to bring other resources to the table that will blend well with the college or university. We call this practice blended management.

—
1

Embracing Change

"Nothing stops an organization faster than people who believe that the way they worked yesterday is the best way to work tomorrow. To succeed, not only do your people have to change the way they act; they have got to change the way they think about the past."
—Jon Madonna, CEO, KPMG Peat Marwick

In 1991, George Mason University (GMU) hired Jeff Brandywine as our chief human resources officer. Today he is the university's special counsel and the key liaison person with the attorney general's office in Richmond, Virginia. In many organizations such a quasi-lateral, quasi-promotional move would have been nearly impossible. The transfer would have been bogged down, if not in the university's own bureaucratic selection procedures, then by those of the central state bureaucracy or the internal politics of the organization itself.

We share this story to show the critical importance of establishing a shared vision of corporate adaptability and agility between the employee and the organization. Our ability to make such an arrangement work, however, is not an indication that GMU has overcome all internal bureaucratic practices and procedures.

This individual came to the university with multiple talents and a diverse set of skills, but most importantly he understood the university's culture of adaptability. Through his insight and his awareness of the direction of the institution, he helped us capture another North Star (guiding light) type when attempting to explain our support service reengineering culture. In every interview with the finalists for the CHRO position, he shared the following synopsis of working at George Mason University:

"Pretty much every morning when I wake up, I can rest assured that I will have the opportunity to make a difference and that is exciting. I am not sure, however, if I will be batting right-handed or

3

*left-handed. If the uncertainty and the normal anxiety associated
with change does not excite you, you most definitely need to look
elsewhere for future employment."*

—Jeff Brandwine, Special Counsel, GMU

That attitude typifies why GMU has been successful to date in its efforts
to transform not only how it provides its support services, but how its staff
and outsourced partners go about getting the job done every day. We have
expanded upon this quote and share it with staff throughout the campus. It is
now understood that:

*"You will also not know if you will be facing a righty or a south
paw; having the wind blowing in or out or from left field to right
field or vice versa; or need a sacrifice, a single or a home run to
win the game. You will, however, know two things: 1. the pitch,
although you may have never seen one like it before, will be one
that if you remain agile and adaptable, is one that you can hit; and
2. if you take your best swing, you may not win the game for us, but
you will be a better player and we will be a better organization by
you stepping up to the plate and taking a swing . . . We only lose as
an organization if we stand there with the bat on our shoulders and
look at a ball zoom by for a called third strike."*

—Creed, George Mason University

Attack with a Passion

As Jack Welch, CEO of General Electric Company, tells his audiences,
"Change is like a steamroller moving at five m.p.h. You can easily walk ahead
of it, but if you stop, it'll run you over." Not a day goes by that an internal process is not challenged. GMU, like any complex organization, struggles to sen-
sitively communicate that this daily challenge is not personal. It is not an
attack on a colleague's professional expertise. We attack every existing pro-
cedure, practice and policy with a passion, but it is always with the intention
of being constructive and contributing to the well being of the greater enter-
prise. The staff must be reminded on a regular and routine basis that this continuous reevaluation and reengineering of the essential support services is
crucial to the effective delivery of the institution's core mission of teaching,
research and service.

Windows of Opportunity—Hallways of Distraction

You must be aware of the pitfalls of continuous reevaluation and self-assessment. The closer you get to the actual service provider the less constructive the self-assessment will seem to the recipient. When we are removed from the actual delivery of the service, it is easy for us to see the need to bring a set of fresh eyes in to help us better focus on the issue at hand. Those who actually toil the soil everyday—your frontliners—are not usually as appreciative of close scrutiny from those without any direct responsibility for the operation. Because you will often be perceived as the intruder, your most important task is to create an environment of trust and honesty. Without this achievement, or at least the acknowledgment of that objective, you will never successfully overcome the natural we-they workforce culture between management and staff. You cannot encourage self-assessment and embrace change if you have not been totally honest with the affected personnel at your institution.

In our president's executive council meetings, one of the responsibilities of the chief university life officer, Karen Rosenblum, is to bring forward three or four items every week that represent complaints or concerns from the students regarding the quality of life on campus. It has been interesting to observe how the initial defensiveness of some of the members of the council upon hearing a complaint in their area of responsibility has softened over the months. However, that initial defensiveness from an executive council member was nothing compared to the initial reaction of the service supervisor when the executive council member followed up on a complaint. And that emotional exchange was absolutely nothing when compared to the exchange between the service supervisor and the front-line service provider.

The issues addressed in our executive council meetings are just as important today as they were yesterday, and our follow up just as speedy. But today the group understands that these issues are intended to help us improve, not to simply criticize.

------------------------------ **Lesson 1** ------------------------

The long term solution to service improvement is not in the actual change incorporated in the service or product being provided, but in the change culture and environment we create between and amongst all those responsible for the delivery of the product or the service.

At any given time, the boss can correct the flaw or malfunction in a system of delivery by simply sending out an edict. The change will be implemented, but the organization has not progressed to be able to solve the next issue that arises. You must give the broader organization (from top to bottom) the opportunity to learn during this resolution-finding activity. Front-line staff often has the best chance to help you keep your eye on the moving targets of service excellence. But they need support from the top to help them keep their senses alert and fresh. Management can help accomplish this by sharing the organizational vision with the staff on a regular, routine basis. The key, of course, is management's capacity to understand and communicate this focus and then provide an environment for its employees to help them maintain mission concentration. The following assessment questions need to be asked:

- Can we as an organization stay focused on the target?
- Can we understand that the target is constantly moving?
- Can we applaud constructive criticism and dismantle the cancerous, ill-intended, backstabbing actions within our organization?

This subtle skill set of distinguishing windows from hallways is nurtured through an organization's ability to identify evasive, ambiguous inter-relationships between seemingly disparate entities. As an institution, we are strong advocates of "consequence critiques," a management concept that requires the identification of service inter-relationships. Once we understand these relationships, we are in a much better position to determine the probable consequences of any service-related decision. The critique of these consequences provides the information necessary to differentiate between "gotta happen" decisions and "no big deal" kinds of choices.

Consequence critiquing improves focus on unit/institution mission and allows us to more quickly locate where we last saw our best practice target the previous day. In the past, it had become frustrating to be unable to find the target today, after having just sighted it yesterday. Now, we understand that knowing where the target was last seen gives us a huge head start every morning on our competition. The sharing and understanding of the vision is our target sighting enabler. That is our advantage! Today, we need only adjust our sights and take aim once again at this elusive target of excellence.

Lesson 2

---------------------   --------------------
Only through sharp mission concentration can an organization distinguish windows of opportunities from hallways of interesting distraction.

Cultivating the Change Culture

Some critics have a name for this type of versatility, agility, and adaptability. They call it chaos—or, on a more generous day, operating without a
strategic plan. We think such critics miss the mark.

What is so exciting about the change culture is the freedom it brings to
match strength against strength—the flexibility of the organization versus the
changing demands of the market place. It is true, however, that you must
make a leap of faith from the comfort zone to the unknown. We have as our
reassurance the knowledge that yesterday's ways will not solve tomorrow's
problems. We can be certain that a strict adherence to a hierarchical organization chart of reporting relationships for critical thinking and decision making
is doomed. Successful organizations know that most opportunities are here
today and gone tomorrow. Only those with the culture (top to bottom) to
respond to these opportunities in a timely fashion will reap the rewards of
responsible responsiveness—the ultimate competitive advantage.

> *"Strangely enough, in the midst of change, the present course may
> often be the most risky one. It may only serve to perpetuate
> irrelevancy."*
>
> —Florida Speaker's Advisory Committee on the Future

This organizational culture keenly acknowledges that there are a myriad
of factors affecting the delivery of products and services that are beyond the
control of the organization itself. No organization is totally and exclusively in
control of its destiny! Having established that principle, the question becomes
not one of determining how to gain more control, but how to develop the best
practices in such a changing environment, thereby ensuring a future in the
market place. This leads an organization to the natural conclusion that:

> *"There will be just two kinds of organizations in the future: smart
> or dead."*
>
> —Randall Fields, CEO Park City Group

Although we have said that this book is about the successful embrace of change, it is really about people, because without their participation there will be no embrace of change. Your investment in your people, and the effort you exert to communicate your concern to them about their welfare is the key to weaving the fabric of culture change throughout your organization.

Lesson 3

No organization can successfully be a change agent in any particular industry or service without a dedicated staff (internal or external) of competent, change agent personnel throughout the organization.

"You have not lived and suffered in vain. What has been must now go. What has gone will rise again. Stop trembling! Get ready to live!"

—Gustav Mahler

To embrace change, colleges and universities must look at the rationale behind their approach for best practices, and that is agility and adaptability. This requires an organizational mentality that is committed to finding the resources when they are needed.

Review Functional Issues

George Mason University is committed to continuous improvement through ongoing functional unit reviews. On a multi-year rotating schedule, all units undergo a critical assessment of their effectiveness, which is a unit review exercise that includes the participation of university staff both internal and external to the unit itself. This has become normal business at GMU. An even more exciting change has been our deliberate commitment to expand these unit reviews to functional reviews. It is no longer enough to know that the unit is operating efficiently and effectively. The focus of the functional reviews has shifted to look horizontally at all interlaced functions, as well as both upstream and downstream at service-receivers, to cover the entire service spectra instead of simply evaluating a singular office.

If there is a weakness in the outcome (product or service), our only chance to correct the situation is to investigate the matter as a functional issue. Some of our most frequently neglected consumers are colleagues within our own organization. The effectiveness of their efforts is often directly related to the quality of the service provided by another division within the same organization. Although it is fashionable to trash the conveyor belt mentality of the automobile assembly lines of the early–mid 20th century automobile manufacturers, some lessons seemed to have been fast forgotten by those of us in the service industry as we approach the 21st century.

- **Lesson 4** -

Even the simplest process is more complicated than the singular sequencing of independent activities. There is never just one assembly line operating. Multiple processes intertwine with each other, but the concurrent sequencing of each process must be orchestrated to provide a high quality service or product at the desired time of delivery.

- -

Poor workmanship early in the sequencing of service delivery, or poor workmanship by one division while working concurrently with another during the same stage of the sequencing of activities will likely result in either substantial rework or a totally unacceptable performance. There are multiple, virtual assembly lines working at full capacity across each of our campuses as we provide our services to the consumer. Our best advice is to never underestimate the importance of the smallest contribution being made by any division.

Parallel Sequencing and Interlacing

The stories at GMU that illustrate this need for orchestration are no different than those on your campus. To be successful in this orchestration, your staff must understand parallel sequencing and interlacing. Parallel sequencing means that for any given outcome to be achieved, several concurrent processes must be in operation at the same time. Interlacing means that each action in the process must occur at exactly the right time—if the action occurs too early or too late, the benefit is lost.

An institution's admissions and enrollment processes provide good illustration of the importance of parallel sequencing and interlacing. To see how these concepts work at your own organization, ask yourself the following questions:

- Do your enrollment management personnel understand, for instance that although the admissions process (its own internal sequencing system), may guarantee an admissions decision in a timely fashion, the actual enrollment of that prospective student is dependent upon several other parallel sequencing activities?

- Does the financial aid decision-making apparatus provide a decision at the right time for the student to make an informed admissions decision?

- Is the prospective student advised in an appropriate time frame of his or her on-campus housing assignment?

- Have you been able to guarantee the individual a single room, if that is what is being requested?

- Has domicile been decided, or will the student be treated as an out-of-state until the decision is made much later in the process?

------------------------------ **Lesson 5** ------------------------

Functional reviews require an in-depth analysis of support service interaction. We must determine the interlacing effectiveness of each support service with other interdependent support service to accurately assess the value of any support service. Effective review and evaluation of complex, interdependent processes requires regular and routine review.

At GMU, a lesson we learned the hard way is that several parallel processes must be in operation as we attempt to attract high quality prospective students. In our case, each unit within the university must understand its importance to the ultimate decision of the student. We need to know what information we must provide and what action we must take to ensure that at the critical moment of decision making the student has all the information necessary to make an informed choice. Can we get our act together? The most important outcome is not whether the student selects GMU. We are smart enough to know that we do not control the actual decision by the student. Instead, we must ask ourselves the following: did we put forward our best effort; and did we provide the student with the total package at the time of decision making? That requires successful parallel sequencing, and that we do indeed control.

If all assignments are carried out in an orchestrated fashion the ultimate goal has an excellent chance of being highly successful. Our support services are no different.

Sometimes, But Not All the Time

When our operations are not running on all cylinders, it doesn't spell immediate disaster. It does, however, mean that our success will most likely rest on the strength and capacity of certain individuals to save the situation.

We all have those special staff members who come to our rescue when something in the process doesn't work. But this kind of rescue will only work some of the time. When interdependent processes are not operating in harmony with each other, the chances for success are greatly reduced. You cannot count on the superhuman effort of a couple of individuals to rescue your operations on a day-to-day basis. The better solution is to dedicate more time to communicate throughout your organization the need for, and importance of, synchronized parallel sequencing and timely interlacing.

The concept of interlacing is most analogous to the inner-cogwork of a watch. It is, for example, the ability of your housing operation to provide room assignments or room availability information when the prospective or returning student needs the information. We must be able to synchronize interdependent operations with distinct and separate missions to reach out and touch one another at the precise time to effect a best practice service.

------------------------- **Lesson 6** ---------------------

Effective service evaluations are not possible unless the performance review includes a value added contribution analysis from the interdependent services that rely on the service being evaluated.

The most recent support service example at GMU has been event management. Being in a vibrant metropolitan, edge-city environment, GMU has always been called upon to host a myriad of community events. Interestingly enough, although our ability to host these events was marked with inconsistency throughout the early–mid 1990s, all of those tangentially related campus offices (Parking, Campus Police, University Relations, Community Relations, Student Services, Intercollegiate Athletics, Admissions, Alumni Affairs, etc.) got high performance ratings in the unit reviews. Our management and coordination of these events, however, was not debatable. We seemed to just barely avoid disaster on a routine basis. Often nothing short of a last minute, superhuman effort on the part of a university staff or contract partner saved the day.

Lesson 7

The underlying problems causing unsatisfactory service performance do not always surface through traditional, organizationally vertical unit reviews. However, during comprehensive, organizationally horizontal functional reviews all weak or broken internal processes should be uncovered.

The less-than-satisfactory critique of our events management certainly should not have been unexpected. Consider these factors: the university was growing quickly; individual units throughout the campus, although enterprising and entrepreneurial, took to the community in an uncoordinated fashion; university resources to support events were limited; the university's telecommunication technology infrastructure to coordinate campus events was inadequate; and the event attendees (the Northern Virginia community) demanded the excellence and first class delivery of significant events to which they had become accustomed elsewhere throughout the region.

The university's understanding of the importance of this type of event and activity helped give the issue the sharp focused attention necessary for taking immediate corrective action. All that was required before embarking on the solution journey was for GMU to confirm the importance of hosting these events at this stage of the institution's development. Since it was essential for this upstart university to own the region, hosting every possible important event was a no-brainer! The following assessments, however, were also determined:

1. Nothing less than flawless event management was acceptable.

2. No singular office within the university organization appeared capable of providing a coordinated solution to accomplishing this assignment (unit issues of territoriality and ownership were in need of demolition).

3. The university needed to make a positive statement to the region to explain both its interest and its capacity to effectively manage events.

The university staff from several of the affected offices accepted the responsibility for delivery of an acceptable solution. Uncertain if any existing personnel could assume leadership in this coordination solution, the university group developed an event management coordinator job description and a search ensued. Much to the surprise of all involved, the best application came from an organization rather than an individual. (Beware: This was almost the end of the story, since personnel folks were initially unable to grapple with handling a corporate application for a staff vacancy. Later Affirmative Action/Equal Employment Opportunity folks became concerned about the legality and appropriateness of the process, and then the purchasing folks became even more concerned with the offer, since the selection had not been processed through the state procurement system.)

All parties, however, came to see the real value of breaking out of the box to find a solution for this particular issue, and as a result GMU can report that events management is now capably managed by an outsourced firm. GMU is still not flawless in its events management. We still don't have enough space to juggle student classroom and laboratory requirements, extra-curricular student events, and those community events of the GMU Center for the Arts (a 2,000 seat concert hall) and the Patriot Center (a 10,000 seat arena), but tremendous improvement has been made. An institutional commitment to develop a pricing policy schedule combined with an adaptable charge-back policy mechanism to differentiate charges to be assessed public service, community education events from those to be charged to the non-affiliated, private or corporate, externally sponsored and funded events was crucial to this improvement. The target goal of community acceptance, and acknowledgment that events at GMU are consistently well managed has been accomplished—at least for the moment.

Lesson 8

Although a bulls eye shot should be applauded, it must also be understood that the target will continue to move and will do so without notice. The quest for best practices is an exercise in rigorous, relentless review and informed decision making.

—
2

Taking Aim: The RFP Process

This chapter explores the process of outsourcing college and university services by providing an in-depth look at the RFP process. Its goal is to broaden your awareness of available opportunities and offer examples of how to do it right and how not to do it wrong. It is not a how-to manual on the development of a request for proposals (RFP). We will share with you what we have learned about the challenges and opportunities associated with the RFP process. Forewarned is forearmed!

To get the most from this chapter, you will need to continue in your mode of rigorous self-assessment and out-of-box thinking for best practices. You will also need to determine if your RFP looks more like a **R**equiem **F**or **P**assivity or a **R**oadmap **F**or **P**erformance. When the market place reads your RFP, will it prompt them to fasten their seat belts and prepare for take-off, or unfasten their seat belts and feel free to walk around the cabin?

When your organization has finished developing an RFP, review it and ask yourself these questions:

- What message are you trying to send?
- Are you asking for creative, out-of-the-box approaches or does your RFP tell potential bidders to simply connect the dots?
- Do you realize that whether intended or unintended, your RFP is sending a message?

------------------------------ **Lesson 9** ------------------------

Remember that for many in the market place, an RFP is their first impression of both your organization and your support services. Pick your words wisely!

Let the Process Begin!

Support services are generally procured either through the issuance of an RFP or an invitation for bids (IFB). The RFP typically will provide more flexibility in choosing a quality contractor. State institutions are often required to provide a written justification before initiating the process, which usually consists of an explanation that competitive sealed bidding is neither practical nor fiscally advantageous to the institution. This review analysis and evaluation, although not mandatory for all institutions, can be advantageous to anyone searching for a best practice.

Do not make the decision on what proposal-requesting vehicle to use before doing your homework. Before you decide whether to use an RFP or an IFB, take the time and effort necessary to evaluate the alternatives.

- Would you be satisfied in awarding this support service contract exclusively on the basis of low bid?

- Do you know all the interrelationships between this support service and all of the other support services that either affect or are affected by the delivery of this particular support service?

All too often, we overlook issues that should have been resolved at the pre-RFP decision stage. Such issues do not disappear, they simply surface much later in the process, often weakening your future negotiating position and unnecessarily lengthening the selection process.

Our advice is that you must be relentless in your front-end support service research. Ask the right questions of the right people. Research is tough! It is a time-consuming, grueling exercise whose rewards (which far exceed the costs) do not become fully appreciated until much later in the selection process. This research is one of the five R's in our formula for satisfactory RFP process progress:

Lesson 10

The more Rigorous the Review and Research, the more Rewarding the ultimate Results.

IFB or RFP?

So how do you decide whether to use an RFP or IFB? These guidelines should help you make your choice:

- Invitation for Bids. An IFB can be used for goods or services that can be clearly and definitively described. The responses from bidders can be matched against the specifications provided. Responsive bids are evaluated primarily on the basis of cost. The evaluative question in terms of low cost bid criteria is responsive and responsible. This type procurement does not include negotiation with firm(s).

- Request for Proposals. This is also referred to as a competitive negotiation process. The RFP process provides the flexibility to describe the desired service or product in more general terms and provides the offerors with the opportunity to suggest more creative approaches. Proposals are evaluated upon a set of pre-determined criteria and weighted factors. Negotiations are conducted with selected offerors. Offers and counter-offers are a significant part of the process, and cost is often not the primary factor in the selection.

Although we most often procure our support services through the RFP process, there are several support services that could, under the right circumstances, benefit from the IFB process. For instance, laundry service, uniform service, landscaping, grounds maintenance, and custodial services are likely candidates at GMU for the IFB process. These are viable services for the IFB procurement process because we have established accurate base-line (operational and financial) information, and we have created easy-to-evaluate performance measures.

As a general guideline, we would choose an IFB over an RFP where we have:

- significant in-house service expertise,

- a detailed knowledge of the service requirements, and

- an informed understanding of the short and mid-range outlook (future) of the respective industry.

George Mason University typically uses an RFP for support services because factors other than cost generally play a major role. With changing technology, we are not always aware of the most advanced range of services the industry can offer at times of rebid. Offerors are therefore encouraged to be creative and are evaluated on flexibility, innovation, problem solving, communication, and commitment to customers. This RFP development process also requires innovation and creativity on the part of the university if a unique approach is expected from the contractor. All old dogs need to learn new tricks—not just the corporate dogs.

The RFP must clearly identify expected levels and quality of service, performance standards, monitoring procedures, relationship between cost and service, termination options, evaluation criteria, and other terms that are specific to the service being outsourced. You must convey your expectations so that offerors can prepare responsive proposals. The RFP should include the operational mission, short and long term service goals, management or operational duties and responsibilities, and any investments required in plant or equipment. This language will provide the framework for contractors to prepare their proposals.

Where you are certain of your needs and how you want the service to be provided, be as specific and comprehensive as possible. Where you wish to encourage innovative and creative approaches, use language that gives offerors the flexibility to float a variety of options.

------------------------------ **Lesson 11** ------------------------------

Share with your prospective partners the historical facts or events that have led you to the point of seeking their interest. This history will often provide invaluable information to prospective offerors.

Make sure to identify future opportunities (i.e., increased enrollment, new buildings, etc.) for improvement, and reveal any known impediments to

Figure 1
IFB VERSUS RFP

Invitation for Bids	Request for Proposals
Competitive Procurement	Competitive procurement (includes negotiations)
Sealed Submissions; Judgmental Factors Limited	Sealed Submissions; Judgmental Factors Evaluation
Detailed Specifications	Minimum Requirements
Evaluate Against Specifications	Evaluate Against Criteria
No Changes After Opening	Discussion/Changes After Opening
Lowest Price Award (Responsive & Responsible)	Price/Quality/Quality Trade-Offs

Source: American Management Association

success. A quick, side-by-side comparison of the RFP and the IFB is shown in figure 1.

RFP/IFB Development Team

The selection of the development team is important. Individuals who understand the operation must join forces with institutional representatives who are willing to learn and serve in a leadership role during the process. Keep the team small—between three and seven members. Larger panels can be unwieldy and make it difficult to coordinate meetings in a timely fashion. Coordinating schedules with more than eight members can become a nightmare!

Invest + Vest = Best!

To the extent possible, use the same individuals who will assist you in the Five Step unit/functional review process outlined in part 2 of this book. This continuity will not only make the process itself more efficient, but these folks now own a piece of the rock. As new shareholders, their initial interest has been escalated to increased service expectations, shared responsibility and performance accountability. This team is the most likely group of individuals to assume, and then retain, a long-term vested interest in the support service.

------------------------ **Lesson 12** ---------------------

The more you provide staff the opportunity to invest time and effort in your search for best practices, the more likely they are to assume a vested interest in the organization. As a team, these staff members will demand and accept no less than a best practices outcome.

Institutional field (front-line) personnel are mandatory when forming the RFP development team. Those most familiar with the service can provide the necessary foundation to develop a comprehensive document that includes a thorough coverage of the more technical aspects of the proposal. Additionally, your team must include an expert institutional contract management representative. This individual must have a complete understanding of the procurement procedures of your organization.

When developing performance specifications, you should look at established industry and professional standards and gain insight from consultation with outside experts in the service industry. If your service needs are complex or unfamiliar, potential offerors may be able to provide helpful information or advice on how the service should be performed.

The benefits of having a mixture of university and non-university team members outweighs the associated problems of bringing together two disparate groups. We have found that it is often simply essential to bring in outside individuals who possess a greater level of industry experience, knowledge, and understanding than the current university staff. With external team participants, one perceived drawback is the mixing of oil and water. Will there be an immediate retreat by team members to either a corporate camp or a university camp? Probably, yes. There will be a natural tendency of some team members to gravitate to one camp or the other. You can mitigate this!

Lesson 13

If the team leader has the confidence and objectivity to help the team distinguish the strong and weak suggestions—regardless of whether coming from an institutional or a corporate participant—the camp mentality will quickly dissipate. This is another opportunity for your RFP development team leader to put into action the concept of blended management.

When including external participants on your RFP team, another potential problem to be aware of is conflicts of interest or issues of confidentiality. If you are not clear in your directions, it is possible (although unlikely) that your selected team members from private industry could pass on information to potential clients or firms that could jeopardize the procurement process. These hurdles can only be successfully cleared if you take the time when establishing the team to explain the rules of the game.

It is often difficult to get outside people, such as professionals in the field, to commit to the time demands of a college or university RFP process. You can alleviate this time demand by maximizing your use of technology (utilizing fax, e-mail, etc.) and using these outside people more like consultants. They can also serve as your safety-net to ensure that you request the doable and release a state-of-the-art caliber RFP. Their external assistance can serve as an informal arbiter to balance the needs of the offeror and the institution. They can remind you that one party typically sees the RFP language as saying "give" while the other party sees the same language as saying "take." A consultant can provide objectivity and balance. A quick way to eliminate interest is to release an RFP that is perceived as one-sided and out-of-balance in favor of the institution. In pioneering-type RFPs, it can be useful to have such a facilitator to keep you from pulling on the rope too hard, and thereby jeopardizing any corporate interest.

Don't overlook potential public sector participants! Several institutions of higher education are just down the road from George Mason University, and many governmental agencies have similar support services. To a certain degree, this is also true of your surrounding local jurisdictions. We have been able to enhance our understanding of our own support services through our relationships with nearby Arlington County, Fairfax City, Fairfax County, City of Manassas, and Prince William County operations. Be sure to check out other similar agencies or organizations in your region. Individuals from these organizations will have much to offer to your process, and they often conclude their contribution to the college or university having not only learned more about your institution but feeling that the college or university has valued their particular professional expertise.

Lesson 14

Take advantage of your natural resources. Discover your diamonds in the rough. No organization can afford to reinvent every wheel in every search for a best practice.

If individuals on the development team do not pull their weight, they should not continue on the RFP development team. Too often a title or position is the sole criteria for appointment. Individuals must have some vested interest if they are to ask the necessary tough questions throughout the process. The development and subsequent evaluation process is too important to involve those who demonstrate little or no effort.

The challenge and key consideration is to select a team that on balance will accurately and objectively assess each delivery system of each support service alternative. Differing perspectives and biases are positive features of such teams, as long as the team as a whole has a balance to its deliberations. During this process we are often reminded that:

"We can have unity without conformity."

—Warren Bennis

At its kick-off meeting the RFP development team should review the existing evaluation of the support service. Additionally, the team should get a full explanation of why the functional review team identified outsourcing as a potential best practice. The purpose of this meeting is to ensure that each team member understands the goals and objectives of the decision-making process and knows his or her individual roles and responsibilities. You must determine if any biases exist amongst the team members that could reduce their objectivity in recommending the eventual decision on how to provide this support service in the future. Do not allow this ultimate decision on outsourcing to become an emotional and biased choice where the facts relative to performance and institutional context do not guide the final decision.

------------------------------ **Lesson 15** ------------------

Take off the gloves early, and do not allow participants to pull their punches. All players must develop a thick skin, and a critical-yet-constructive mindset. Your team must have the capacity to weather the stress and complexity associated with decision making at later stages of the process.

Survey and Focus Group Input

At George Mason University, we feel it is important to include as much customer service evaluation information in the RFP as possible. This customer information obtained through surveys, focus groups, and interviews with various constituents should be made available first to the RFP development team and then to prospective offerors with the release of the RFP. These surveys have been useful because they assess the existing effectiveness of a variety of service issues across the campus. Information from focus groups tends to be even more effective when advising potential offerors of specific issues, because focus groups usually offer more in-depth information than provided in support service surveys.

Language: Asset or Liability

Any overly ambiguous language in the early draft of your RFP must be questioned and clarified throughout the entire process. If the reason for the ambiguity is that the institution does not understand its own requirements, then it certainly will not be able to communicate them to an outside provider. Keep in mind, however, that conscious ambiguity can be an invitation for creativity on the part of the offeror. Sometimes you will consciously decide that ambiguity is your default parameter. If you are willing to consider different approaches to meet your requirements, let it be known that you are open to creative and innovative approaches. All parties will benefit from this honesty!

Invitation for Innovation

If you are looking for an innovative approach to your support service, you must understand that such creativity will require some encouragement from you. You can be the creator of innovation by developing a creative pro forma system of delivery in your actual RFP, or you can select RFP language that encourages creativity in the offer. Our student account collection contract and our custodial services contract provide two good examples of the value of creating and soliciting innovation.

SUB2 = Innovation Creator: Student Account Collection

In traditional fashion we established a firm's ability to collect a high rate of past due funds as our key factor in our selection decision. It was also important to us that the selected firm collect funds in a business-like manner that was persuasive but not overly aggressive or abusive. Customer service was a very important factor in the collections process. We looked at degree of automation, resumes of staff committed to the contract, professional association affiliations, proposed collection fee process, and any past or current legal problems. We also asked for copies of the literature, letters, and notices the offeror sent to student debtors. In traditional offer review fashion, we then rated the offers based on qualifications, knowledge, and experience in that particular market place. Everything about our process looked like anyone else's RFP for student account collections.

However, we also introduced innovation into the process when we used RFP flexible language that allowed us to award two separate collection contracts, and then flip-flop the agencies every semester from primary to secondary. This strategy has been a successful move to encourage collection agency competition and earnings while maximizing results for the university. We had determined that with only one agency, the service provider often becomes complacent. This complacency seemed to remain equally probable even with a fixed primary-secondary arrangement. Under our rotating strategy, both agencies are fully aware of the arrangement and understand that we will naturally compare the results. This is a unique arrangement since it is customary for most universities to follow the fixed primary-secondary model without the flip-flop. This strategy gives two competing firms their day in the sun as the primary collection firm on a rotating basis each year of the contract.

Innovation Solicitor: Custodial Services

Providing custodial services at the newly constructed Johnson Center gave us another opportunity to test a creative outsource approach. GMU's Johnson Center is a an integrated library-student union that opened in 1996. Our physical plant staff could not easily estimate the type of custodial tasks and frequencies required to meet the needs of the building, since we had no custodial service history for this unique type of facility and were unable to establish its projected utilization. Under some circumstances, this could have been problematic. The pioneering concept of the building, combined with its special character and the need for it to succeed conceptually, demanded the development of an RFP with an innovative approach to providing support.

In procuring this custodial service, we needed to use RFP language that would encourage an innovative approach because our objective, and the only acceptable level of initial custodial service, was a level that would generate immediate, unconditional, unsolicited compliments from the visiting public. This was a level of custodial service without precedent at GMU, and probably in most public institutions. It was the concept behind the building that was really being tested, and we were not willing to risk an objective evaluation of this facility concept by providing less-than-satisfactory custodial support services.

Thus, the selected contractor would need to demonstrate a willingness to be flexible through the early stages of the contract and provide just-in-time custodial service by continuously adjusting its corporate processes to meet a yet-undefined service demand. There would be several periods of service adjustment as we attempted to reach the right level of custodial support. To the extent possible, we had to include calibration language in both the RFP and subsequent contract. The demonstrated flexibility of offerors and their ability to provide high quality customer service on demand was a predominant factor in that award process.

Lesson 16

You will usually pay extra for language ambiguity, but conscious ambiguity is occasionally the best tactic to pursue when you are clear about your ultimate objective, but you are unclear about the best approach.

Lesson 17

The final calibration of support services can only be accomplished after the service objective has been determined within the context of the core organization. You need to be willing to adjust your calibration on a regular basis if you are attempting to develop/maintain a leading edge organization.

Innovative Performance Measures

In support services with easily quantifiable performance measures like grounds maintenance and housekeeping, you must eliminate unnecessary ambiguity in service requirements. Additional as-needed services or add-ons such as event set-ups or special event ground maintenance should not be left unaddressed. These costs and performance standards must be carefully spelled out in the specifications. Module specific language can also be particularly effective for specifying different levels of service for multiple facilities combined in one contract. Too often, what we do not tell the offerors in the language of the RFP will only surface later during contract negotiations or disputes. Don't default to over-generalization in your RFP when you know you need differentiation in your service levels.

For example, one custodial contract at our Fairfax campus covers 24 administrative and academic buildings, but service levels vary by building. Some buildings require a higher frequency of custodial tasks, and certain facilities, like the Student Health Center, require a hospital standard level of custodial service. Other custodial contracts on campus call for the prestige standard and those are generally associated with special event facilities such as the Athletic Field House, Child Development Center, and Center for the Arts. Sometimes we are not smart enough to put this differentiating language in our request for services. In these situations, it is not unusual for potential offerors to raise this issue after we have already released the RFP. Although their question may come as a surprise or maybe even an embarrassment, there is no need to panic. Time is always on your side. What is critical is that when an organization is asked for a more definitive explanation of any of its service specifications, you (A) take the time to determine and communicate the varying levels of service being requested, and (B) ensure that all potential offerors receive the same clarification at the same time.

Lesson 18

Keep the playing field as level as possible. Every institution must have a formal process in place to ensure that when questions are raised by prospective offerors, all potential offerors receive a timely clarification to ambiguous language.

Determining variations in the levels of service and frequency of service should always be a deliberate decision by the institution. These decisions on standard of care and appearance are institutional statements of priority. They are not physical plant or building management decisions. Therefore, take advantage of the institutional breadth of your team. Senior management concurrence is generally advisable.

We have found that once we have established the custodial service performance standards, the issue of contract compliance can become problematic. Our most effective strategy for continuous satisfactory service performance is to make sure that our service customers (the occupants) know the levels and frequencies of services that have been contracted on their behalf. This information in the hands of the actual customer improves tremendously our capacity to effectively monitor the progress of our corporate partner.

Outsourcing Ownership

We have learned that where you have a feeling of facility ownership, you very rarely will have an ambiguity issue in special event support service requirements. In these more clearly defined facilities, you will have someone on your campus with a passion and a sense of ownership about the building and how it is maintained. Specificity of support service requirements will not be a problem in these facilities. However, ownership of the general classroom buildings is often not as clear in terms of institutional ownership and that can be a problem. The evaluation of those service contracts for general use classroom facilities is no less critical in terms of subcontractor relationships, evaluation of satisfactory performance, and time limits for correcting deficiencies than your university-owned type facilities.

You must define institutional ownership and accountability in your RFP. Assign this task to an individual with the knowledge, interest, and passion necessary to seriously engage in this contract management. Your contract management is doomed if your system assumes that responsibility for successful service rests solely with the RFP-designated official university contract administrator. Effective contract administration is network sensitive. The better your first-line field personnel know the terms of the service contract and are part of a dynamic communication process with the university contract administrator and the service provider, the greater your chances for satisfactory contract performance.

------------------------------ **Lesson 19** --------------------

If there is no strong ownership in the process, or if there is no one in your organization with a passion about qualitative or quantitative objectives of the service, you will most likely receive proposals that match your perceived interest in the service.

Focus on Your Conceptual Driver

The outcome of the outsourcing can result in cost savings, increased revenue, better management, or a myriad of other financial and programmatic benefits, but you should never lose sight of your conceptual driver. Our conceptual driver is usually increased customer satisfaction and overall improvement in the quality of services provided by the institution. In more than 50 privatization ventures, George Mason University has seldom reduced actual operating cost as a result of outsourcing, but we have always improved the bottom line quality of service. We tend to improve the financial bottom line because our improved quality of service has tapped lost revenue opportunities of the past.

Lesson 20

When looking for new ways to provide support services that are not the core activities of an organization, service improvement is more likely to be found in discovering new revenue opportunities than through cost containment measures.

You may have, however, uncovered through your unit review that a particular support service is not only providing unacceptable service, but is also doing so at a higher than acceptable cost. If this is the case, your focus is dual-pronged as you aim for improved customer satisfaction and an actual reduction in the cost of operation. The key is to make this clear in your RFP. A short history of this support service on your campus in the language of your RFP can be very enlightening to prospective offerors. The conceptual driver that has led you to this review of outsourcing is never as obvious to the general public as you imagine.

Lesson 21

Cut to the chase early and often. Share what you are looking for, why you are looking for their interest, and how their assistance may enable you to better achieve the vision of the organization. Do not put all the good stuff at the end of the RFP.

Best Practices—No Bars Held

If your conceptual driver is best practices, you must consider service elimination as a possibility. If as an institution we decide that either we cannot provide the level of service that we find necessary or we do not want to expend the required time and effort on such an activity, elimination of the service may be the best practice.

On occasion, the decision to outsource is a statement that the institution does not want to exert the energy to provide the service itself. As discussed earlier, there are many reasons to consider outsourcing, but sometimes colleges and universities decide it is just not worth the effort to do it in-house. If this type of analysis happens on your campus, just getting out of the service totally may be your best move. For example, having a self-operated ice cream shop or a recognized chain as your on-campus service provider may be the best way to provide the service on your campus. However, at some colleges or universities the best practice may be to discontinue the activity and advise students of nearby off-campus ice cream shops.

---------------------------------- **Lesson 22** --------------------

In searching for best practices, consider the possibility that the service itself should be discontinued.

Modular Outsourcing

In some situations, you may determine that there are several distinct services within a traditionally more generalized support service. We have found that modular outsourcing has proven to be a successful alternative to contracts of comprehensive campus exclusivity. To pursue this strategy successfully, you must carefully select and then distinguish your mandatory requirements for each subservice within the umbrella service RFP. This also gives firms the chance to pick and choose from your menu of subset options. By using clear and concise language, you can usually accommodate both the large firms and their comprehensive exclusivity interests and the smaller firms with their more specialized perspectives.

The inclusion of terms requiring significant capital renovations can essentially eliminate many outstanding small businesses from submitting a proposal on that particular module. Are you willing to set the financial investment requirement at such a level that all young entrepreneurial firms are eliminated? An affirmative answer to this question may lead you to a most effective strategy. We only caution that you fully understand the consequences of setting such parameters. With the module format, you may get the best of all worlds. You may decide to blend some young firms with some more established firms providing different-but-related sub-services, thereby providing the perfect mix to accrue the greatest benefit to the institution.

If you are serious about modular outsourcing, you need to be cognizant of the expanded performance evaluation efforts required of your staff. Our prime example of modular outsourcing is our food service partnership. We have determined over the years that we have 12 different subsets of our food service operation, which we review as interdependent elements of the overall food service operation.

As you can see from the evaluation form, shown in figure 2 (overleaf), we evaluate each of these subsets on five different factors, with each factor having four separately evaluated service features. This $12 \times 5 \times 4$ perfor-

Figure 2
CONTRACT EVALUATION—FOOD SERVICES

Contract Administrator: (enter name here)_____

I. FINANCIAL FACTORS (to be completed by contract administrator)

	Gross Sales By Area (%)	Change From Prior Year (%)	Net Income ($)	Comments
PW Campus				
Arlington Campus				
Fairfax Campus				
Bistro				
Crossroads				
JLC Food Court				
Ciao Hall				
LaPatisserie				
Equivalency				
Board Plan				
SUB I				
Catering				
Convenience Store				

II. PRODUCT FACTORS

	Price	Choice/ Variety	Quality of Food	Comments
PW Campus				
Arlington Campus				
Fairfax Campus				
Bistro				
Crossroads				
JLC Food Court				
Ciao Hall				
LaPatisserie				
Equivalency				
Board Plan				
SUB I				
Catering				
Convenience Store				

Figure 2 (continued)
CONTRACT EVALUATION—FOOD SERVICES

III. SERVICE FACTORS

	Hours of Operation	Promptness of Service	Accuracy of Service	Responsiveness to Dietary Needs
PW Campus				
Arlington Campus				
Fairfax Campus				
Bistro				
Crossroads				
JLC Food Court				
Ciao Hall				
LaPatisserie				
Equivalency				
Board Plan				
SUB I				
Catering				
Convenience Store				

IV. PERSONNEL FACTORS

	Knowledge-able	Courteous	Effective Communi-cations	Professional Appearance
PW Campus				
Arlington Campus				
Fairfax Campus				
Bistro				
Crossroads				
JLC Food Court				
Ciao Hall				
LaPatisserie				
Equivalency				
Board Plan				
SUB I				
Catering				
Convenience Store				

Continued overleaf

Figure 2 (concluded)
CONTRACT EVALUATION—FOOD SERVICES

II. FACILITY FACTORS

	Cleanliness	Ambience/ Eye Appeal	Comfort and Size	Convenience of Location
PW Campus				
Arlington Campus				
Fairfax Campus				
Bistro				
Crossroads				
JLC Food Court				
Ciao Hall				
LaPatisserie				
Equivalency				
Board Plan				
SUB I				
Catering				
Conv. Store				

VENDOR RATING FACTORS (to be completed by vendor)

	Sales (Increases)	Sales Per Labor Hour	Return to Both Marriott & GMU	Food Safety Score Sheet
Overall Operation				

	Accident Rate	Mystery Shopper Evaluation	Corporate Comparative Rating
Overall Operation			

ADDITIONAL COMMENTS

_____
_____
_____
_____
_____
_____
_____
_____

mance evaluation matrix is the basis for our review of each element of the food service contract. In addition, we utilize seven corporate performance indicators that we have determined are equally meaningful to the institution in our annual assessment of the effectiveness of the service partnership.

Roles and Responsibilities, Part I

Performance specifications will describe the standards by which a service can be effectively measured, but you must be explicit in specifying what the parties can expect from each other. The institution must provide clarity in the RFP on the responsibilities of each party. Your specifications must be clear and provide enough detail so that offerors will know exactly what is provided by the institution. These performance specifications are the tools which will help us measure the quality and effectiveness of both the service and service provider. For example, we found that throughout all components of our student housing operation, we needed a clear division of responsibilities between the parties. That includes residential life, maintenance, security, custodial, laundry, and grounds services whether outsourced or in-house. You must specify in the RFP the relationships that will be required and the overlapping duties and responsibilities with other service providers such as parking, food services, university police, and the physical plant department.

In 1995, student housing had become a support service operation of significant concern at George Mason University. We decided to look at off-campus models that might be able to attain better service results and generate greater residential student occupancy. Basically, the institution wanted to see what, if anything, the private sector could bring to the table. We had already outsourced the housekeeping, building maintenance, and grounds maintenance of student housing, but we knew outsourcing the actual day-to-day operational management would be both pioneering and risky. After significant consultation with the housing staff at Georgia Tech, we issued an RFP for comprehensive management of student housing. The language of the document seemed perfectly clear that GMU wanted a firm with a corporate attitude that the student was a guest, and that facility standards would be established to be equal to those provided by hotel management for all of their guests. We used our 2×12 role and responsibility matrix model similar to the one shown in figure 3. where we identify the 12 most important activities and assign responsibility to one of the two parties.

Figure 3
ROLES AND RESPONSIBILITIES MATRIX
Activity: Housing Management

Selected Functions	Primary Responsibility	
	GMU	**PARTNER**
1. Marketing	X	X
2. Room Assignment		X
3. Custodial Services		X
4. Grounds Maintenance		X
5. Insurance Coverage	X	
6. Price Setting	X	
7. Emergency Response	X	X
8. Parking Coordination	X	
9. Deferred Maintenance	X	
10. Routine Building Maintenance		X
11. Discipline	X	
12. Room Damage Assessment		X

However, what wasn't so clear was the delineation of roles and responsibilities of the partners in certain subactivities within the activity of university life. One of the first problems we discovered was that the RFP did not clearly explain who would be responsible for first line response to student behavior issues. Although we had committed several pages of information in the RFP to discussing this item of a rapid response system, the combination of the numbers of possible student incidents and the type of response necessary while operating a student housing system were nearly infinite. Rather than attempt to list all potential incidents, we should have adopted an umbrella like philosophy that provided broader guidance to the contractor.

Another issue that surfaced in the same contract occurred when the new contractor began referring to the newly selected, corporate student residential staff as Student Service Representatives (SSR). Most new and returning students understood the long-standing title of Resident Assistant (RA), but seemed confused about the title and role of the SSR. We used RFP language that made it clear that the contractor was responsible for the employment of these student assistants, but we did not foresee the need to address who was responsible for naming these student positions. We advised the contractor to change their title back to RAs the next year. You can never anticipate everything that might arise during a contract, so aiming to develop a line-item, all-inclusive RFP is a misguided objective.

Lesson 23

Where the partnership is understood to be a pioneering venture, there should be sufficient policy guidance supported by an adequate system of checks and balances to keep either party from wandering too far astray.

We also had to revisit our original assumption that guest status was the right service target, because the transition students complained that they wanted something different than guest services. They wanted the feeling of security and protection combined with the high visibility of a friendly RA. They didn't want concierge service; they wanted to know there was someone nearby to handle the day-to-day issues of students sharing living space.

Lesson 24

A shot that misses the target is nothing more than a temporary setback. It is one of the natural consequences of taking a shot. Our ultimate objective in such instances is timely recovery. This recovery, however, can only take place if we check out the first shot at the target. As necessary as a second shot may be, it should not be taken until we determine what caused the first shot to go astray. We must continue our listening and learning to make the second shot a smarter shot!

Both parties must know how the relationship will be managed. If performance measures have been built into the request for proposals, there should be no surprises later. The best way to ensure effective management of your contracts is to set reasonable but specific performance standards in the RFP. The best-monitored contracts can typically be traced to clean, concise performance indicators in the language of the RFP. Lack of success in contract management is often directly related to failure to identify those performance standards in quantitative terms.

When writing the RFP, standards can be categorized as mandatory or desirable. Mandatory specifications describe tasks that the institution requires for a minimally acceptable level of service. An offeror's failure to meet these RFP requirements may cause you to determine that its proposal is non-responsive. The use of desirable standards can serve to establish an additional range of criteria that may be of value to you when comparing competitive offeror proposals. However, you should limit your use of desirables. Almost by definition, your desirables will send a mixed message to prospective service providers.

Lesson 25

If the item is important to you, make it a mandatory requirement. If it is something that you simply consider desirable, leave it to your prospective partners to address the issue in their actual proposal. Their initial position gives you another chance to see if you and your prospective partners are thinking similarly.

Roles and Responsibilities, Part II

Retain what you want to maintain! Never delegate complete authority over those activities that can irreversibly tarnish your institutional image or reputation. If you see an action or activity as encompassing broad institutional policy matter, you must retain substantial, if not exclusive, authority. For example, with food services, George Mason University retains total control of pricing, which means we must do the necessary homework to make wise pricing decisions. You might ask, why control pricing? We believe pricing is more about institutional policy than revenue generation. We also believe that pricing of room and board rates is a critical factor in the selection of a college or university for many prospective high school graduates. Whatever your institutional philosophy on pricing, it is important that you address pricing control responsibilities in the RFP.

If you wish to retain pricing authority, you must understand the elasticity of pricing in each of the food service outlets. We review individual profit/loss statements from each food unit to make informed pricing decisions. We receive invaluable pricing information from our corporate partner. When a college or university offers multiple food options on campus, it must insist on financial statements that provide management information so intelligent decisions can be made on the profitability or non-profitability of each different location and each different food service format. Without this information, you become overly dependent upon the perceptions and bias of the contractor and lack the necessary data for informed decision-making of your own. This is not to suggest that pricing is an issue that requires institutional control on every campus. Only the institution itself can determine those issues of institutional policy for which it shall retain authority.

You must, however, never lose sight of the fact that you and your corporate partner have different reasons for being. You both have different visions of the world. What you hope to accomplish through your partnership is a mutual understanding that it is in the best interest of both parties to blend particular expertise together to attain a shared mission. Our best shot at success comes from our capacity to enter into an agreement on how we can share responsibilities to attain a set of shared goals and objectives. We will be most successful in this venture when both parties realize that our shared mission is consistent with both of our visions.

------------------------------ **Lesson 26** ------------------------------

Every partnership must embrace the concept of shared responsibilities and a shared objective. The more effectively the partnership achieves the shared objective, the more expansive the definition of shared responsibilities will usually become. However, in all partnerships there are certain decisions for which one party must assume ultimate responsibility.

RFP: The Document

Protection is important. You are looking to form a mutually beneficial, long-term relationship between your college or university and a corporate service provider. A key to the success of such a venture is the level of trust between the two parties. Another critical factor is the institution's commitment of time and effort to performance review and regular, routine communication. To facilitate successful partnerships, our RFPs always provide institutional access to the audited financial statements of our corporate partners. Although this access protects the interests of the institution, it is seen (and explained by the institution) much more as an essential resource to the parties for meaningful financial dialogue. Without this information, it is near impossible for two parties to understand the respective financial position of each other relative to the contract.

Lesson 27

Full disclosure of pertinent financial information will never harm the trust factor within a partnership. A reluctance to share such information should be a cause for some concern. Trust is built on sharing, not withholding. Partnerships do not prosper with blind faith. Blind faith is just that! Blind.

Proportionality is important. If a student housing RFP has 25 pages on facilities management and three on university life, the contract will be a facilities management contract. Whether this was your intention or not, that will be the perception of all interested parties. Is that how you want your request to be perceived? On other occasions the weighting criteria in an RFP will be the heaviest in the customer service features, but the entire narrative may appear to be financial in nature. This confuses the prospective offerors, but probably leaves them with the perception that this is a financial-oriented contract, not a service-oriented contract. When you dedicate the bulk of your RFP document to what you know about the service, but not to what is of primary importance to you, the best you can hope for is misguided confusion.

One of our classic miscues along these lines was our original housing RFP for total operational management. Since we knew the most about financial and facilities management, we dedicated three-fourths of the document to these issues—even though our primary objective was to find a corporate partner to help us incorporate housing into the fabric of university life. Since we did not know how to accomplish this objective, the RFP included little reference to this aspect of managing student housing. What we received is exactly what the market perceived we were requesting—property management proposals.

Lesson 28

Do not dodge the unknown, especially in your more pioneering requests for service partners. Where it is unclear to you how to achieve your service achievements, you must let your prospective partners know that you are "looking" and that you are not locked into a specific system of delivery.

Even when you think you know everything you need to know about a particular support service industry, allow for some flexibility in your RFP. In the following two examples, we found out the hard way that what we thought we knew just wasn't the way we thought it was:

For our residential laundry RFP, one offeror strongly recommended increasing the number of machines, which would have required a significant investment. He also recommended increasing the vending price. The offeror said that this combination would result in higher revenue and more satisfied students, and in return the offeror requested a long-term contract. This was a non-negotiable position of the firm, since it was the foundation-setting philosophy of all of its corporation operations.

The university balked at the proposal, however, because we were looking more narrowly at the out-of-pocket cost to our students. We were getting a reasonable return as compared to industry standards, and we had a three-year contract with two one-year renewals. The RFP had made it clear that we would not award a contract with a term greater than five years. The corporate offeror on the other hand had never entered into an agreement of less than five years, and 97 percent of the firms' agreements were seven- to ten-year contracts.

We did not listen to their message, and they did not make a very quantifiable, persuasive argument. In retrospect, it became clear that their inability or unwillingness to quantify the benefits associated with a longer-term contract increased our resistance to entertain the lengthy multi-year proposal. It is possible that each party assumed that the other fully understood why they held their particular philosophic position, so neither expended the energy necessary to effectively communicate their rationale. As a result, both parties probably missed a golden opportunity. Today there does seem to be evidence (under the right contractual terms) of substantial quantifiable benefits associated with lengthier laundry service contracts.

Lesson 29

Avoid all-knowing language! Even where you feel the most competency and use the most precise language, you must present yourself in a way that gives the prospective partner the freedom to challenge your position. Any potential partner understands that making such a challenge is risky, but you should regard this challenge as a last gasp opportunity to reassess your position.

In our amusement game IFB of 1997, we required one high volume change machine with a capacity of $5,000. One year after the contract was awarded, the contractor had still not supplied the change machine and was six months behind in revenue payments to GMU. Because the company failed to respond to contract requirements, the university terminated the contract. In the next IFB, the university once again emphasized its requirement for one high volume change machine to be supplied by the contractor with the capacity to hold $5,000. This time, however, offerors were quick to inform GMU that there was no such thing, and that the maximum capacity at the time was $1,500. Ouch!

Lesson 30

Get your act together! Prior to hitting the street you must aquire an indepth knowledge of the service by researching industry trends, standards, and current capabilities.

Weighting Evaluation Criteria

You must establish the right performance evaluation weights. Selection criteria can include quality of service, responsiveness, financial stability of the offeror, design of facilities, staffing and management plans, completeness of the bid, operational cost, experience in providing service to similar clients, etc. Other criteria can be customized to a particular service area such as turn-around time, staff commitment to the contract, and understanding the institution's goals and objectives for the operation. Corporate flexibility is often important, and in some support service areas the contractor must have the capacity to change operations in a timely fashion due to unforeseen circumstances. If that is what you anticipate as your need in a particular support service, you need to give it a high evaluation weight.

Lesson 31

Why are you looking for a partner? You must determine what is most important in your selection of a partner. Assign criteria weights to accurately reflect what is of greatest importance to your organization. If a particular criteria for selection is to carry the freight, give it the weight.

Do not be reluctant to (a) establish the desired characteristics of your service partner, and then (b) evaluate the corporate-like culture qualities of each offeror. These are the core qualities of the competing firms and you can effectively research these during the selection (reference check) process. This character reference investigation is no less important for corporations than for individuals. Use the language of the RFP to tell prospective offerors what you are looking for in a corporate partner. It is reasonable to ask, What kind of character is this corporation?

Lesson 32

Do not interject any cute innovative mathematical point systems when developing your formula for weighting selection criteria. Do not confuse your partner at this juncture. Simply give the greatest weight to the criteria of most importance to you and make it perfectly clear.

Changing Times: Changing Criteria

You cannot afford to copy someone else's weighting criteria, and you cannot afford to simply use the same weights today as you used in your last RFP for this same support service. For GMU's beverage RFP in 1994, evaluation criteria were 40 percent for providing the service and quality product brands and another 40 percent for financial return to GMU. Only a 20 percent weight was attributed to other support (financial or non-financial) offered to the university. In the second RFP document, which was drafted only months after the first RFP process had to be prematurely terminated, the criteria was changed to provide a weight of only 25 percent for product brand plans and service; and another 50 percent weight for financial return. The weight given for additional contributions such as scholarships or support of athletic programs increased to 25 percent.

We changed the weights between the first and second RFP because we learned during this short interim period that the product brand and service plan was not going to differentiate any of the offers. Although the measure of quality of product and quality of service plan remained important, we knew the ultimate decision would be based on distinguishing the financial and non-financial return to the university. We decided therefore to give a greater weight to these two criteria.

Lesson 33

Weight each selection criteria to facilitate the eventual differentiation
of competing proposals.

Often a less-than-satisfactory service contract experience will help you
learn and enable you to craft smarter language into future RFPs. With one
banking and cash management contract, service to GMU had been so unsatisfactory that customer service became the overriding concern in the next bid.
In 1989, RFP criteria contained strong financial considerations, while a 1994
RFP gave the greatest weight for qualification and relevant experience,
understanding required institutional services and plans, and past corporate
success. In addition to increasing the customer satisfaction criteria from 60
percent to 80 percent, the university incorporated quantifiable service measures throughout the RFP document. (See figure 4.)

Another example of how changing times can affect needs has been the
history of our bookstore contract. The language in our 1984 bookstore RFP
was simple and straightforward. We were looking for a contractor to direct,
manage, operate, and generally provide bookstore services on-campus. We
were concerned about the cost of goods and percentage of used books sold,

Figure 4
GEORGE MASON UNIVERSITY: BANKING SERVICES
Changing Times: 1989 Criteria Versus 1994 Criteria

RFP 1989		RFP 1994	
Financial Conditions	20%	Financial Conditions	10%
Favorable Cost/ University Return	20%	Favorable Cost/ University Return	10%
Staff Commitment	20%	Understanding Required Services and Specific Plans	40%
Timing of Services	15%	Qualification and Relevant Experience	25%
Specific Plans	10%	Past Success	15%
Participation of Small, Women, and Minority-Owned Businesses	10%	Favorable References	5%

but criteria was 70 percent for performance of services and financial considerations.

In 1989, the RFP format changed completely and focused on the role and purpose of a GMU bookstore in university life. George Mason University was looking for complete and comprehensive bookstore services, improved revenue, and a high level of service. The criteria now included experience in providing bookstore services, technical expertise and credentials of personnel, favorable references, and a record of high quality of service. We also added the need for increased service hours, improved mix of goods, shorter lines, and more flexible payment plans.

By 1994, we shifted emphasis and encouraged offerors to design the interior of the new bookstore and make it an exciting and special place in a new and innovative building. We knew what we could expect in terms of a financial return so that was no longer the distinguishing criteria. We were looking for more than a bookstore. We were looking for a partner who would grow and change, adapt to new situations, and meet challenges that did not even currently exist.

By 1999, it was clear that this new bookstore partner would need to be a firm that embraced change. Internet sales needed to be seen as an opportunity, not a threat. We were looking for a corporate partner with a vision of the campus bookstore of the 21st century.

Lesson 34

There are no boilerplate, off-the-shelf short cuts to partnership excellence. Yesterday's lines of courtship (an old RFP) will not serve you well in attracting the interest of future partners.

Lesson 35

When searching for a partner, give yourself and your partner a chance to learn as much as possible about each other. Use essay questions rather than true/false or multiple choice questions.

Pre-proposal Conference

Any pre-proposal conference will give you an early look at the quality of the potential offerors before you receive their proposals. Therefore, our advice is to always include RFP language that establishes either an optional or a mandatory pre-proposal conference. Mandatory conferences tend to send a signal as to the seriousness that you attach to the service and this will be perceived in such a manner by all potentially interested parties. Although you are still in the RFP development stage, you should remind the entire team that this pre-proposal conference, as well as any possible site visits, is a major marketing event for the institution.

If the delivery of the service is complex, uncertain or likely to change, you may have trouble describing service delivery expectations with any great specificity. In such cases, a mandatory pre-proposal conference often will given potential offerors more insight into the particular service by providing you the opportunity to clarify or elaborate on the RFP. A pre-proposal conference (optional or mandatory) is a fact finding and explanation session only. You should always offer a site visit opportunity to your particular service operation. We tend to make such a visit optional, but we always encourage offerors to get better acquainted with the service. This is a marketing opportunity and should not be done in a slip-shod manner. For those firms that are interested, we have tour guides available and prepared.

Lesson 36

You only get one chance to make a first impression. Do not get caught napping!

RFP: Marketing the Institution

The RFP is a selling document and not just a buying instrument. Every RFP must be marketed even when an institution is totally satisfied with its current contractor. You must guard against RFP language complacency as well as body language complacency, especially where you have a longstanding outsourcing partner. It is easy to be passive when everything seems to be operating smoothly. Additionally, getting too comfortable with your current corporate partner will be readily perceived by potential competitors and that can be a serious detriment to you in your pursuit of healthy competition.

Marketing should reflect the market place. For instance, our parking service RFP process benefited from our urban/suburban location. There were a number of interested firms and many firmly established companies operating parking structures. Parking management was the lifeblood of those firms, while parking service management was not remotely close to the core mission of the university. There was good competition, and we knew of these companies' interest to expand into higher education. Our marketing efforts were minimal but effective.

------------------------------ **Lesson 37** ----------------------

Effective marketing requires that you mark the market before you embrace any particular marketing strategies.

If companies are not expressing an interest in your RFP, it could be for a variety of reasons. For example, companies many think the institution is satisfied with its existing contractor and decide not to waste their time. It could also be due to a changing market where there simply are fewer firms providing a particular service. Corporate firms are very carefully selecting the service areas they enter as well as the RFPs to which they respond. Do not underestimate the time, effort, and cost of submitting proposals—whether or not to respond to your RFP is a corporate decision of significant relevance. Your RFP language, your pre-proposal conference, and your telephone inquiry response system will either attract their interest or dissuade them from submitting a proposal. Nothing you do at this stage of the process goes unnoticed. Perception is reality!

An institution must engage in active recruitment of attractive offerors. Put on your Sunday best! Look at industry trends and best practice providers of the specified services and start courting them.

Marketing your support service request is essential under all circumstances. The extent of your marketing should reflect the market place, but it is a mistake to assume that you are dealing with a captive audience. The RFP package must be attractive and you need to present yourself as a quality product and a wise investment. If your homework has been done right, there should be no great surprises or disappointments in the proposal response rate to your RFP.

> *"Competition is the engine that creates the savings and efficiencies . . . by itself it does not yield annual operating savings. It is the change in organizational performance which results from being subjected to a competitive environment that yields the savings."*
> —Virginia Commonwealth Competition Council
> Annual Report, 1997

Do not be surprised if your institution finds itself with very nominal interest in its RFP. You should see this train coming down the track. The language of your RFP should protect you from a weak market response. If you decide upon a corporate partner in a weak market environment, you should have a flexible termination provision in your contract. You should also incorporate a successor clause to cover any potential future corporate buyout. Be mindful that a weak response to your RFP has not weakened your position. This is no time to begin compromising your demands.

------------------------------ **Lesson 38** ------------------------------

Don't even go there! Do not negotiate any organizational non-negotiables, even when there appears to be very limited interest in your request. A one-horse town doesn't mean that you have to ride that horse. You always have a choice. You can go it alone, if necessary.

In-house Competition

You should encourage and sometimes demand in-house institutional service proposals. First you must assess the internal atmosphere for bids or rebids. There are times when you must require an internal bid. For example, where an outsourced service has been repeatedly criticized by university support service staff, it's time to see if your complainant can become your next support service provider. Another time to ask for an in-house proposal is where the service is currently being provided by an effective university staff, but you have determined that it is necessary to look at other service delivery alternatives. Finally, if an adversarial or even highly competitive atmosphere has developed between a contractor and self-operated service staff, the internal staff must be given a chance to bid on the service.

At a minimum, when you anticipate being faced with a non-competitive environment you should circle the wagons and take a hard look at self-operation. Consider hiring an outside consultant to assist the in-house staff in developing a plan to self-operate the service. Occasionally, your particular situation (size and experience of staff) does not lend itself to the development of an internal proposal without outside assistance. Do not miss a shot at a best practice because you are reluctant to hire a consultant to assess your in-house operational capabilities.

Lesson 39

At every critical juncture of the process you must review your options. Time affects the viability of your choices. There are no time constraints on checking in to reassess your latitude and longitude.

Mental Mythical Model

Whether we anticipate nominal or substantial competition, at GMU we develop a three M's strawman strategy: a Mental Mythical Model with all the attributes we hope to receive in an offer. This mythical strawman may not represent real competition, but it helps us maintain focus on what we originally expected from this undertaking. That constant reminder has been invaluable to us in all RFP processes, but especially when we find ourselves in fairly non-competitive environments.

We have had situations where we have received only one response to a service RFP. Instead of panicking, we continued discussions with the sole offeror and compared their corporate responses to our three "M" strawman. That process has allowed us on several occasions to enter into a partnership that bore a much greater resemblance to our mythical strawman than the offeror's original proposal.

Catch the Fever

There aren't many more exciting days in support services than the due date for respondent offers to your RFP. Make it a special event for your RFP development team. A little beverage and snack gathering is a nice way to get the team together as the offers are recorded with your official business representative. Unless your situation is much different than ours, you can expect a flurry of submissions just before the deadline. If you have created the desired level of excitement within your team, they will be as anxious as plaintiffs and defendants waiting for the jury to return with a verdict. This can be a memorable moment. Take advantage of the bonding opportunity!

You can expect a surprise. You may get an offer from a firm that you thought had become disinterested. On the other hand, you may be disappointed by the absence of an offer from a firm that you thought would submit a competitive offer. Although your emotions will be running high, this is also a day of strict adherence to the rules. We have had corporate representatives miss the proposal submission deadline by less than five minutes, and we have had others tied up in traffic less than a mile away from campus. If you have incorporated mandatory submission deadlines into your RFP, there is no room for compromise at this particular moment of the process. Deadlines are either met or missed. You must turn control of the process over to your official business representative who will most likely be your expert material management/procurement officer.

You can be confident that your official business representative (the sheriff) will be surrounded by plenty of competing corporate representatives (self appointed deputies) with bids already submitted to assist you in your strict enforcement of the rules of the game.

Lesson 40

From the earliest moments (pre-conception) of a partnership search, you must develop your rules of engagement. Adherence to these rules by both you and your potential partners is non-negotiable. There will be no party favors during this search for a partner.

Responsiveness: Go or No Go

You must determine responsiveness shortly after acceptance of the offerors. At this point in the process, the development team, most likely led by their official business representative, must review each offer for responsiveness. You must determine if the offer meets all your RFP mandatory requirements. This first gate screening is a mandatory step in your offer review process. This is primarily a technical task, but if you have included mandatory program requirements in your RFP, each offer must specifically address your requirements. If an offer does not satisfy your requirements, you may determine the offer to be non-responsive. Although your rules of engagement will differ from state to state and between institutions, you most likely have the authority or responsibility to reject non-responsive proposals from further consideration.

At this stage you are determining offer responsiveness, not proposal attractiveness. This distinction is of monumental importance. It is essential that your material management/procurement representative guide you through this stage of the process. You must make a decision on responsiveness at this point, and the decision will be irrevocable!

If you are considering any changes in personnel between the RFP development team and the RFP evaluation team, you need to keep the RFP development team engaged through the responsiveness analysis of the offers. We strongly recommend that for purposes of continuity, you maintain a high level of personnel consistency throughout the process, but sometimes because the team players have other time commitments, you may have a higher than desirable turnover rate. Since continuity of team personnel is a significant advantage to you during this process, you may increase the probability of maintaining team chemistry by making the anticipated time commitment known to all members early in the RFP process.

The key is that the RFP development team must complete your responsiveness screening. These team members understand both the intent and the letter of the law as it relates to the actual language of the RFP. This review for responsiveness should be accomplished as soon as possible after receipt of the offers. We have found that a simple check list is usually all you need to accomplish this task. Additionally, each element included on the responsiveness worksheet should have a RFP section and page citation for future reference. Once you have developed a uniform check list and have it approved by your official business representative, the team reviews each offer to ensure responsiveness.

Lesson 41

Although the actual responsiveness analysis can only occur after the offers are received, the responsiveness scorecard should be developed before the RFP is released.

Determining responsiveness will not be as simple as you anticipate. For example, with each of our custodial RFPs over the past 20 years, we have seen great disparity in the cost estimates of the offerors, despite the fact that these costs are based on identical specifications. Such wide variations in cost estimates should be a responsiveness red flag to any institution. You must, at least momentarily, assume that the variance could be attributable to a failure to respond to all the facets of your service request. In 1991, an IFB for custodial services of one building ranged from $7,900 per month to as high as $14,000. In a 1995 procurement, there was a $100,000 variance between a low custodial bid of $467,000 and the next lowest bidder! For that same procurement, bids were as high as $976,000 with the average being $700,000. For our most recent Arlington campus (one building) custodial IFB, bids ranged from $48,000 to $106,000.

Lesson 42

In determining responsiveness, you must begin peeling the layers off the onion. You must find the reasons for variances between competing offers. When faced with significant variances in proposals, your follow-up analysis must include a rigorous review of the financial assumptions being made by the offerors.

One financial example of a potential finding of non-responsiveness was our recent landscaping IFB for athletic fields. The apparent low bidder had almost an 80 percent difference in cost for the services. It appeared that we had a bidder that misunderstood the request. We had received 12 bids on this project, and the other 11 bids were very close in their cost estimates. Every early indication pointed toward a non-responsive low bidder. On further investigation, we learned that the low offer had come from a contractor who was providing grounds maintenance services for adjacent varsity athletic fields just off campus. This gave the firm a substantial competitive advantage because it was able to avoid relocation and mobilization costs of both equipment and personnel. In this case, discarding the dramatically low bid as non-responsive would have eliminated a best practice offer.

Lesson 43

When determining offer responsiveness there is no short-cut around an in-depth proposal content review. Closely check out the scope!

The responsiveness analysis also provides a financial insurance policy. The analysis is aimed solely at determining the responsiveness of the financial proposal, not the attractiveness. This determination is priceless, because it relieves your evaluation team of the need to engage in a similarly detailed investigation. The insurance policy assures the evaluation team that they have an apples-to-apples comparison. As illustrated in our athletic field grounds maintenance example, you may find the mother lode in a low bid that is outside the tight bidding range. You don't need to think about throwing it away because it looks too good to be true. You can now rely upon the earlier finding of responsiveness as an initial reference point. Your evaluation team has a certain level of assurance, but when the proposal is actually handed off to them it will be time for them to get down and dirty. The responsiveness check doesn't relieve the need for further evaluation, but it ensures you that you are not wasting your time on a non-responsive offer. The evaluation team must now determine if that great looking offer is a diamond or cubic zirconia.

------------------------- **Lesson 44** --------------------

Strong competition alone does not ensure a complete understanding of your support service needs. Not even a tight grouping of financial proposals should give you great confidence.

Offer Acknowledgment

When you have determined the responsiveness of the offers, we recommend that the university respond to each submitting firm and officially advise them of receipt of their offers. Any information you can provide at this point about your anticipated time schedule, will be greatly appreciated by the offerors. This acknowledgment is not only a gesture on your part that recognizes the time and effort that each of these firms exerted, but it also says something about the class and style of your own institution. Make a quality statement about your organization. Don't use an out-of-date form letter, printed on the cheapest stock paper in the university inventory, and signed by someone totally unknown by the offerors.

Once you have determined responsiveness, the RFP evaluation team turns its attention to measuring the comparative attractiveness of the offerors. Your RFP should have encouraged contractors to advise you on what is available and what they can provide you to help guide you to the desired outcome. You should closely review each offer to differentiate between those firms submitting an off-the-shelf, cookie-cutter approach from those seriously interested in your particular venture. We have received proposals that inadvertently failed to insert the name of George Mason University and contained the name of another university. Beware of boilerplates!

Much can be learned by what offerors do and do not say when addressing certain specifications of your RFP. Offeror responses often tell you what is important to the offeror by the style of their narrative. For instance, a response that focuses primarily on cost containment can tell you a lot about the character of the corporation. You will find many other tips in their response language to help you distinguish isolationists from those firms who see a broader picture. Some will include control oriented language while others will use collaborative language. All will talk of true partnerships, but many will use language that paints a much different picture. Read between the lines and read the fine print.

Gap Analysis: Gap or Gaping

The most effective way to evaluate the attractiveness of each offer is to conduct an institutional expectations gap analysis of each of the offers. When the gap analysis is concluded, the RFP development team will have begun the ranking/scoring phase of the process. State rules and regulations may dictate your specific options at this point, but generally the team will determine whether offers have gaps or gaping holes.

1—Gap Most aspects of the offer are in the ballpark. However, the offer either does not fully address a critical element of the request or answers in a manner that we have determined to be less than totally satisfactory. We shall proceed to request additional information for clarification.

2—Gaping The offer is generally unattractive. There are either gaping holes in the firm's responses or gaping differences between its offers and our expectations. We may proceed by requesting additional information but we are more likely to determine the offer unacceptable for further consideration.

It is important to remember at this juncture that you are in the driver's seat. This gap analysis should help you begin differentiating the attractiveness of each offer. Your gap analysis can leave you with an unacceptable non-financial, gaping hole determination just as easily as a financial gaping hole finding. The following is a recent GMU gap analysis example:

With parking services, corporate expertise and the strength of each of the offers was much different than what we had expected. We requested a comprehensive offer to manage all aspects of our parking service division. The offers attempted to address our needs, but each offer made it clear that their strength was effective parking lot/deck management with a control culture of constant enforcement. We were requesting contractors to manage our entire parking operation, not just the operation of a parking deck, and this was foreign to many prospective offerors. Each offer was weak in the area of university parking service management. Their parking industry experience was familiar with enforcement issues for cars that are locked in a deck and cannot get out, or for cars that are illegally parked and need to be towed, but we were asking for multiple university parking-related services.

Each parking contractor knew how to run a deck structure, but none had ever managed in a campus culture environment with the daily issues surrounding student and faculty parking. Needless to say, these firms had little experience in handling eminent faculty violators. Through our gap analysis we quickly corrected our preconceived notion that any corporate firm could advise George Mason University on all aspects of operating its parking business. We learned through the gap analysis that if we pursued any of these offers, we were entering the blended management cycle as soon as we began this partnership. There would be a steep learning curve for the corporate partner, and the first year would be spent acclimating the contractor to the university environment and the university to the corporate way of doing business.

Through gap analysis we learned that the corporate offerors were bringing a more narrow expertise to the negotiating table than we had originally anticipated. We decided to accept this as "in the ball park," and continued with the selection process. This gap analysis understanding put us on early alert that we would potentially be entering into a partnership that would require extensive culture guidance from the institution. We learned that comprehensive university parking service management was not available in the private industry market place. The gap analysis provided the kind of just-in-time learning that is essential as the RFP process maneuvers around unanticipated occurrences.

Lesson 45

The greatest impediment to progress is not ignorance, but the illusion of knowledge.

With the conclusion of your thorough gap analysis, you are now ready to trim your roster down to your finalists. To some extent, since you know nothing more about these firms than what they have written, this is like a blind date. Your great advantage, however, is you know more about these corporations than you ever knew about a blind date.

Lesson 46

Trust your informed judgment and that of your team. Are you still
excited? If you lost your enthusiasm, it is probably time to regroup and
rethink. If, however, the offers have been responsive and have either
kept or expanded your interest, continue with the selection process.

3

Hitting Your Target: Best Practice

"What gets us into trouble is not what we don't know, it's what we know for certain that just ain't so."

—Yogi Berra

You have written a dynamite RFP. You have taken the time to market it well, and you have received a number of responsive attractive offers. Your RFP evaluation team must now assume the role of manager of a major league baseball team during spring training. Like the baseball manager who must assess the quality of the team roster, the RFP evaluation team must evaluate the quality of the proposals. This chapter illustrates the scoring system we use at George Mason University to evaluate RFPs and explains the steps involved in finding the most responsive RFP and turning it into a signed contract.

Initial Scoring of Proposals

During the scoring stage of the RFP process, each member of your RFP evaluation team will assign an evaluation score based upon the attractiveness of each proposal. The assigned point system should be developed in accordance with the evaluation criteria in the RFP. For each of the subjective evaluation criteria, the best proposal receives the highest (not necessarily the maximum) points for that subjective criteria according to the evaluator's judgment. Although the scoring of points for criteria other than cost is usually a matter of subjectivity, team members' judgment must be based upon the facts as presented in the proposal. An offeror should not be penalized for lack of experience with your institution, but should be judged, on the relevancy of experience and expertise wherever gained. Likewise, an offeror should not be given an unfair advantage or points simply because of a previous contractual relationship with the agency. However, the relevancy of the offeror's support service experience needs to be judged. Points should not be manipulated to favor a preferred supplier, and should be assigned in an impartial manner.

To improve the objectivity of our evaluations, we have found that it is helpful to develop a sequencing evaluation matrix for each member of the team. Scoring and evaluations tend to reflect whether the proposal being graded was done first or last by the evaluator. So mix it up! A sequencing matrix prevents all members of the team from reading the same proposal first. A sample of our sequencing matrix appears in figure 5.

When all team members have concluded their evaluations, one consensus evaluation form should be prepared showing as a minimum: (1) names of the committee members, (2) names of all offerors including those removed from further consideration, (3) evaluation criteria and maximum point values for each, (4) scoring of each team member, and (5) average of points assigned to criteria of each offeror. Individual committee members' written comments and points assigned should be included in the consensus evaluation file summary.

Based on the selection criteria included in the RFP and the evaluation team's consensus score, the team should select two or more offerors deemed to be fully qualified and best suited among those submitting proposals. Each of the finalists should then be interviewed.

At this point, your team will be engaged in several subsequent scoring activities. For instance, each offeror's proposal will be rescored after the interview. This will allow you to determine which firms if any you wish to further consider through the subsequent negotiation stage. You will do your final scoring after the negotiation stage, and the ultimate decision to award will be based on the rescoring of the final negotiated proposals in accordance

Figure 5
SEQUENCING EVALUATION MATRIX

	Order of Reading/Evaluation, Proposals A through E				
Reviewer	**A**	**B**	**C**	**D**	**E**
Clark	1st	2nd	3rd	4th	5th
Meyers	2nd	3rd	4th	5th	1st
Moyer	3rd	4th	5th	1st	2nd
Smith	4th	5th	1st	2nd	3rd
Steele	5th	1st	2nd	3rd	4th

with the evaluation criteria in the RFP. Once you have completed your initial scoring, you are ready to interview your top finalists.

Selecting Finalists

Once the finalists have been identified, the real in-depth research begins for the RFP evaluation team. Don't necessarily believe all that you read. This is a good time for representatives of the RFP evaluation team to visit some of the places identified as references by your offerors. These site visits have proved helpful to us because they allow the subsequent interviews to take on a new level of mutual understanding. Pre-interview site visits have occasionally allowed us to make a more informed decision on whether to continue consideration of a particular offeror.

How often do we award contracts without ever really interviewing the company? The answer is an unqualified never. You would never hire an individual for a position having only read his or her resume. Yet often, costly contracts are awarded without ever really interviewing the contractor. You need to get a real feel for the company with which you are about to partner. Questions should be directed to offerors, responses should be documented, and then you should redirect for clarification until you are satisfied you understand their position.

In 1995, we scheduled housing interviews with the top three offerors. The successful offeror sent several well-informed professional representatives, but one unsuccessful bidder sent a single representative who was nonchalant about the entire process. One-person presentations must overcome the appearance of a mom and pop operation. Despite the fact that no other such contract had been awarded anywhere in the country, he walked in, set down his briefcase, and asked the group to throw questions at him. Many things were thrown his way, but questions were few and far between. Sending several company representatives, preferably with the necessary level of expertise demonstrates a willingness on the part of the contractor to engage in meaningful dialogue.

GMU's experience with interviewing mail service respondents provides a good example of how important the interview of contractors can be. The successful mail service presentation was given by a senior corporate manager, a sales manager, an account manager, and a postal analyst. All questions were answered thoughtfully by this group, and each representative spoke to his or her area of expertise. Another finalist for the same RFP brought four individuals whose roles were not clear. The committee perceived that their attitude was condescending and sometimes arrogant. The firm was overly critical of the university's current mail operation and one of the company's representatives loudly chewed gum throughout the presentation. Although the firm looked fine on paper, we found this lack of respect for the university to be unacceptable. The interview was invaluable to us in reaching this conclusion.

Although an institution can sometimes assess the importance being given its RFP by the level of management the respondent sends to the interview, be wary. Make sure you not only meet the executive level of the corporation, but the level of persons who will actually work on your account. Many colleges and universities have been wooed by the highest levels of a corporation, but never see these people again after the award is made.

Presentations are very important and the presence and absence of particular corporate representatives certainly make a statement about the offeror. In some cases, we have had as many as eight company representatives in the interview room who appeared to have never met each other much less discussed the proposal beforehand. At times, you may find it effective to limit the number of people who represent the firm. You can also request that the firms concentrate on introducing the individuals who will have direct involvement with the contract. When an institution will become the flagship operation or the largest client of the offeror, you can generally anticipate more personal attention and involvement from the firm's senior management. As a rule, when teams or tiers of informed corporate representatives attend the interview, it can be seen as both a compliment to the institution and a message that they have determined that your business is important to their company.

Lesson 47

Evaluate substance, not style. Measure each prospective partner's understanding of your organizational need, not the number of business suits in the room.

It is often important to determine the firm's commitment to your region of the country. Being the offeror's only client in a given region can be problematic unless: (a) you are being touted as their show account, and (b) you are convinced of their interest in the region. You must determine what other contracts they have or are currently pursuing in your geographic region. Even if you are their first venture in the area, they should be able to share with you their corporate strategy in your region.

Lesson 48

A successful show account proposal requires a persuasive "show me" presentation. The talking (proposal) is over; gotta be able to "walk the walk."

The finalists for our 1980 food services contract included big name contractors and a handful of smaller offerors. A less-well-known, out-of-region smaller firm was seen as a greater institutional risk than some of the other more recognizable big name corporations. The smaller firm's presentation, however, was so personal and exuded such a commitment to high quality service that the evaluation team (after completing reference checks and site visits) recommended that it be awarded the contract. The administration, with assistance from the senior management of the small firm, presented a similarly strong submission to our board of visitors which resulted in the board's approval of the selection of that firm. The firm never disappointed, as it established the GMU account as its pearl.

For the 1984 bookstore presentation, another small firm won the hearts of the evaluation team as most of its management organization showed up and convinced us that GMU would be the jewel in the crown of this firm's family of clients. The thrust of that presentation was that the company wanted to grow with George Mason University and that we would become its premier, prototype client. The firm's presentation led us to overcome our concern that it had no other accounts in our region. It presented the following information:

- As a small college service bookstore, they convinced the university to look at their other regions with only a single store. They provided documentation and made a presentation demonstrating how a single store in an area is still supported as well as any other store in the company.

- They convinced the university they were committed to making this isolated store the flagship of the company. They backed this up with the following commitments:

  ✓ They would assign a district manager to run the store on a daily basis rather than a local manager.

✓ They made a commitment to bring technology to campus with the introduction of the country's first electronic textbook ordering system which was designed for the faculty.

✓ They assured the university that their manager would have complete authority over the store budget process. This meant the store would be able to pursue its own destiny rather than rely upon other stores.

• The president of the company promised that he would personally be on the George Mason University campus to see that these things would happen. He provided the university with the necessary personal and corporate assurances.

The firm was awarded the contract.

With the most recent beverage process, we had to overlook the successful offeror's corporate headquarter representative and rely more on the strengths of the regional corporate staff. The corporate headquarters representative strongly inferred that GMU should consider itself fortunate that this beverage firm even submitted a proposal. It is important to know who is and who is not going to be important to your account. We were smart enough to look beyond the shortcomings of personalities within the larger corporate organization.

Lesson 49

You should not be overly influenced (positively or negatively) by players who are not going to have any influence on the eventual relationship.

In George Mason University's 1989 landscaping IFB, our language contained a very detailed work specification and a provision that the respondents would provide references for maintenance of recreational sports fields and facilities. Although the low bidder had provided satisfactory work to the university in the past, we were not convinced that it had retained the necessary depth of specialized experience required for our new sport specific field maintenance. Site visits proved our suspicions to be correct. Clumps of grass and pools of water were evident on the baseball field of two of the reference sites that we visited. That company's bid was rejected and we selected a firm where the site visits produced evidence of the quality workmanship that we expected.

Universities must decide on the compatibility of the best offeror with the institution. This is not a time for compromise. What we have learned over the years is that sometimes you just remain uncertain after the first interview. Often this is not even realized until subsequent interviews with other competitive offerors have been concluded. You may then realize there are holes in the information you gleaned from certain early interviews. Most RFP evaluation teams will naturally improve their interviewing prowess the more they experience actual interviewing. Therefore, do not be surprised if some of your early interviews turn out to be somewhat incomplete. Team interview notes may also be less than totally clear, or the team may decide that it is simply confused by the answers received in a particular interview. No need to panic! Pause, rewind, and play it again, Sam!

Lesson 50

If you remain uncertain about any terms of a particular offer, embark upon a follow-up means of clarification with the offeror. Do not be reluctant to schedule a second interview.

The best advice that we can share is that if you schedule a second interview, you should share the specific rationale for the interview with the firm in advance of the actual follow-up interview. The second interview has proven to be very valuable to us on several occasions, and you will find the offeror both eager and appreciative of the opportunity for clarification.

During a finalist interview for mail services at George Mason University, one firm's presentation showed a serious lack of understanding of university residential mail service and the offeror had difficulty providing any relevant experience in this emerging service. Although the firm had excellent non-university mail service credentials, we felt the potential learning curve would be too steep. The interview was instrumental in making this determination. We selected the firm for a second interview to provide it the opportunity to illustrate preparedness to enter into the institutional mail service market. With its national mail service credentials, the firm deserved our continued consideration and the chance to persuade us of its state of readiness. The second interview did not remedy the shortcomings, but we were much more comfortable in the decision to discontinue our consideration of the offer.

With another mail service firm, the focus seemed to be more on GMU accommodating the firm's special type of operation rather than them accommodating us. There was also a certain rigidity in the firm's employment/hiring policy which would have negatively affected our current employees, including our student workers. The feeling prevailed in the team that the firm would make only marginal changes in its current operations to meet our needs. None of this information could be gleaned from the initial reading of the proposal. As a result of the follow-up interview, the offeror again scored poorly relative to corporate compatibility criteria. Saved by the interview again!

The successful mail service offeror's presentation and interview were hand-tailored to the GMU community, and the firm had a wide range of universities and colleges as current clients. Their willingness to design an operation to meet our needs illustrated a commitment to becoming a partner in this undertaking. Through the interview, they made the choice easy.

Lesson 51

No organization should expect to alter or change a prospective partner to become what the organization needs. Avoid the near-impossible task of changing the culture of another; select the firm with the corporate culture that most closely meets your organizational needs.

Disparate Organizations: Partner Friendly?

When our corporate partners fully understand the concept of blended management, they begin doing things that raise the eyebrows of our own university bureaucrats. We must make sure that we do not let our own outdated policies, practices, and procedures obliterate any chance for the concept of blended management to succeed.

For instance, when your partner begins to buy into the larger, greater organization by donating time, effort, or dollars to other university initiatives unrelated to their particular contract, this gesture should be celebrated, not attacked, by organizational procurement and contact compliance staffers.

- Why would any institution want to disregard such acts of a true partnership?

- How many procurement officers today refuse to give any credit to such parties in their subsequent competition for award or renewal?

- Why do university officials often view these outside-of-the contract activities by our partners as suspicious, tainted or inappropriate?

When your food service partner sponsors a minority affairs speaker series, celebrate the moment. When your bookstore makes a major contribution to your cultural arts performance series, let them know how much it means to the university. You should give full corporate credit where it's due. A firm that has contributed assistance to an institution beyond the terms of its contract has determined that such an investment is a wise business decision. That kind of business partner always deserves a second look. Partnerships and blended management can only succeed if we are institutionally proud of the relationship and proud of the contributions made by our partners. Any such corporate contribution should be widely communicated and applauded throughout the university.

Lesson 52

When selecting a new partner, it is essential that adequate weight be given to each prospective partner's corporate family-giving culture. You must determine your partner's understanding and commitment to total partnering. Will they be a letter or spirit of the law partner?

Don't Ignore the Warning Signs

As mentioned earlier, GMU awarded its beverage contract to a large firm, in spite of some misgivings we had about the representative we met with from this firm's corporate headquarters. A serious problem of internal corporate communication within this firm was detected during the interviews—and this proved to be only the tip of the iceberg! About 18 months after award of the contract, the firm's corporate office surprised us by informing us that it did not have a contract with GMU. This communiqué from corporate headquarters shocked the regional corporate people almost as much as it stunned GMU personnel. A review by legal counsel determined that a binding contract was indeed in place. In this particular negotiation, we ended up dealing with essentially two different levels of the same corporation, and the right hand did not always know what the left was doing.

---------------------------   **Lesson 53**   ---------------------

During the courtship stage you are very possibly seeing the best that
your potential partner has to offer. Your offerors are in their show-time
mode at the interview stage of the process. It is a mistake to assume
that communications will improve after a contract is signed.

Another example of testing compatibility and flexibility was in the interviews of travel firms. We wanted a travel agency operation on campus, and
we understood that our level of business travel was barely adequate to support
such an investment by an agency. To accommodate the desires of the university and the needs of the travel agencies, we agreed to install telephone lines
for on-site agency associates to handle GMU business travel inquiries as well
as the firm's prestige level accounts. Additionally, GMU agreed to promote
the on-campus agency for all the personal travel needs of our university community. The contract incorporated language that gives GMU business travel
the highest service priority. We negotiated hard to attain the on-campus travel
agency because we knew that our GMU travelers had a strong preference for
dealing first hand with on-site travel personnel. This non-negotiable feature
allowed us to determine during the interview process which of the travel firms
was willing to develop a creative partnership arrangement that would provide
us this essential feature and still be mutually beneficial.

-----------------------   **Lesson 54**   -----------------

As you are concluding interviews, remember to:
        ✓ Review your objectives.
        ✓ Maintain your focus.
        ✓ Look for your best partner.
        ✓ Be willing, if necessary, to regroup.
        ✓ Keep your dreams alive.

You should be sure that the following questions have been answered:

- Can you create a definable link between your objectives and the
  responses?

- Do the core competencies the company brings to the table improve
  the university's chances to achieve its mission?

- Considering the proposal(s) that have been made, is there an identified and fully understood linkage to the other inter-related university services?

- Will the acceptance of the offer positively affect the university community?

- Are you comfortable that you have attracted a partner who understands your objectives and is capable of delivering?

If the answers to these questions are yes, continue to move forward and zero in on your best practice partner.

Reference Checks

Your institution should rigorously investigate the lost contracts of each finalist as well as the firm's submitted references. You must check out situations where the firm either lost a contract or was unable to gain renewal of an existing award. You must balance what you hear through references and site visits with the overall track record of the firm. More weight should be given to their most recent contract activity. Look most closely at a trend analysis over the past 24 months. Look for changes in senior leadership.

Reference checks can be conducted before or after the actual interview, but they are crucial. You must insist upon some dialogue on both strengths and weaknesses in every reference check you make. In addition to a site visit to an offeror-recommended reference, you must consult with institutions where the contractor has previously worked that were not provided as references. Additionally, the team should check out a non-referenced institution where the offeror is currently working to determine satisfaction levels with the services being provided.

In these reference checks your institutional support service staff should also speak with these clients of the offerors. Your support staff will often be better able to elicit responses indicative of the firm's understanding of the more detail-oriented nuances of the service. Interviews with on-site contract administrators should result in a good gut feeling for the firm's commitment to customer satisfaction and corporate adaptability. Your task here is that of an investigative reporter. The reference checks must be combined with a thorough site investigation. During this review you should investigate the length of time the contractor has been in business, validate the financial condition of the firm, verify national and regional customers, confirm tenure of key management personnel, and review the contractor's experience with college or university accounts. This will require a considerable amount of staff time and energy, but without completing this task you are assuming their self-acclaimed success is accurate, which is like playing Russian roulette.

We conducted extensive reference checks on each selected travel agency finalist following the firm's presentation. One reference client even shared some information on its negotiation experience with a particular offeror. The tip helped us better understand the corporate culture of the firm. All comments were positive about its service levels, technology, cost savings, and its minimal need for contract supervision. More importantly, the references were eager and willing to talk about the firm and volunteered information that was not requested. An animated give-and-take telephone conversation is often indicative of sincere client satisfaction. References who are difficult to reach or are reluctant to return calls usually indicate an underlying problem that may be hard to unearth.

Lesson 55

The best references are those that go beyond the all-positive response and try to share some balance by providing examples of concerns, issues, weaknesses, or any minor glitches experienced with the prospective partner.

With our mail services RFP, reference checks told us exactly where we should expect to be one year, three years, and five years after signing the contract. The transaction is now complete, and we are almost exactly where we were advised we would be. We have a management fee that has increased overall operational costs higher than our in-house operation costs, but our postal savings have more than offset that cost. Our reference check clients advised us that we should expect this to be the result. Use references to reinforce your positive or negative beliefs.

For one major custodial contract where references seemed a little shaky, one call to a client where the contractor claimed to clean 72 bathrooms revealed that 50 of them were state park-like outhouses that only required once a year cleaning. Despite these and other misrepresentations, however, the contractor was the low bidder in this IFB process and we awarded the firm the contract. Unfortunately, we didn't heed the obvious warning signs. It seemed we could not pass up what appeared to be a great financial deal. Serious service deficiencies have caused multiple complaints from the university occupants throughout the life of the contract.

------------------------- **Lesson 56** -------------------------

Since most references are reluctant to share many problems with you during this review, it is important that when you uncover such concerns, you (a) assess the honesty of your prospective partner relative to this item, and (b) determine the importance of this new information. At a minimum you must shift gears and proceed with increased caution. Remember that's the devil shouting "no fear."

Once you conclude the interviews of the offerors, it is important to pause to reevaluate and review the currency of your initial objective in the review process. Does it appear that further consideration of the outsourcing offers will improve your probability of attaining your desired outcome? The question of whether to continue to pursue the outsourcing offers should be answered through informed evaluation of all the circumstances that surround your particular service on campus and the attractiveness of the offers that you now have before you. The answer to the question of why to consider outsourcing will not, and should not, be the same for each of your support services at each of your campuses. Remember that markets continue to change and an institution must be prepared to regularly evaluate both the outsourcing and the self-operation option. Make sure that you remind yourself that most support services require considerable institutional coordination with other services on campus. Are any of these offerors going to help you improve the essential integration and coordination of these interrelated support services?

Your ability to attain first hand knowledge of similar contracts held by the offeror at comparable contract sites is desirable. You are well advised to look at as many of the contractor's facilities at other locations as possible. Following our travel agency presentations, a group of GMU employees visited the local offices of the two finalists and met their staff members. Then four of our employees joined one firm's account manager and site-manager on a trip to their corporate headquarters in Philadelphia. The visit to their corporate headquarters proved to our team that the offeror had an access to technology that no other offeror could match. Despite the fact the firm is the fifth largest in the world, the firm's president took the time to talk to the evaluation team about the firm and the importance of the GMU contract. Not only was the president a very dedicated, customer-oriented leader, but the employees all looked happy and committed to the same vision espoused by the CEO. The entire trip was a win-win for the firm and its high score for compatible corporate culture was a direct result of the site visit.

Reality Check

At this point in the process, you should take sufficient time to ask yourself again, Should we do this? The decision to outsource has now been enlightened by the additional knowledge you have gained throughout this selection process. How well will the needs of your customers and the needs of the institution be met if you award a contract to one of the offerors? You must determine if the potential offeror can improve the effectiveness of the support service. Here is our series of "must answer yes" questions:

- Is the potential for attaining your service objective enhanced by pursuing this partnership?

- Have you assessed all the possible adverse consequences associated with this partnership?

- Are you confident that the potential negative consequences are more than offset by the advantages associated with this mission-consistent opportunity?

- Are you convinced of the value of this venture? Specifically, has there been sufficient competition to assure that you will get a good product at a fair price?

- Do you have or are you willing to establish the necessary institutional infrastructure to provide the essential oversight to ensure contract compliance and service performance?

Lesson 57

Since you know your organization, it is paramount that you assess your ability to effectively blend together your players with those of each potential partner to improve the delivery of your service.

Trimming the Roster: The Second Cut

Now that the interviews are over and you have decided to further pursue the outsourcing option, you must rescore all corporate firms and decide which ones to further negotiate with. This is your second round of scoring. Since you now have the advantage of the interview, we call this our P3 (people plus paper) scoring round. The key element in this round of institutional scoring is target proximity. Each of the offerors has submitted a proposal, made its most persuasive oral presentation and provided the necessary references to confirm its claims. Which proposal comes closest to hitting your target objectives?

For the most part, you have seen the best they have to offer. It is now time for you to make your next move in the process. Select the proposals and the firms that come the closest to the expectation target that you established at the beginning of this selection process. You should be in an excellent position to make this choice.

Take Your Best Shot

Before you even begin the negotiating process you must have an agreed-upon fall-back strategy. Here are a few things to keep in mind: negotiations are a statement of your priorities. Make the distinction between must haves and niceties. If you cannot come to agreement with your preferred offeror, you must have a Plan B. This will keep you from ever signing an agreement with the feeling that a gun is being held to your head. There is always another option.

Lesson 58

Keep your focus and never waiver on knowing the difference between what you can give up and what is not negotiable. Remember that these negotiations (pre-nuptial agreement) continue to provide insight on the wisdom of a particular partnership.

A well-prepared RFP will strengthen your negotiating position. A hard and fast rule is that an institution must negotiate within the terms of the RFP. Negotiations should always involve more than one bidder unless there is a clearly only one acceptable offeror.

Normally, it is best to assign one person on the evaluation team to be the lead negotiator. Preparatory notes should be made of issues likely to arise during negotiation and plans made to deal with them. You should insist on dealing with someone in full authority to commit the offeror. Parameters of discussion for each point must be established, with the most important issues identified first.

Lesson 59

Prior to the actual negotiation both parties must determine and fully understand the issues to be discussed during negotiations. You cannot expect a fruitful outcome to your initial negotiations if you have not given your potential partner(s) the opportunity to review the issues, determine their position, and develop their negotiating strategies.

Additionally, this communication allows the parties to agree upon the appropriate point in time for the introduction of each of these issues during negotiation. Items of confusion beyond the scope of the RFP should be resolved as early as possible and prior to the actual negotiations. The parties should be encouraged to engage legal counsel to resolve any issues outside the scope and language of the RFP.

You must reassess your original negotiating position now that you have determined which offers are most attractive. The volume of information gained throughout the process is one of the biggest reasons behind the need for reassessment. We have developed an Acceptable Multiple Performance Scorecard (AMPS) to assess the existing attractiveness of the offers as well as the additional voltage we hope to gain at the conclusion of our negotiations. Typically, this scorecard establishes the acceptable scoring range for our highest priorities. These priorities can be traced directly to the original language of the RFP. Each priority in the RFP has been weighted based on importance. The AMPS generally illustrates that the most important priorities have the smallest range of acceptable variance. A sample AMPS appears in figure 6.

As shown in figure 6, this minimum acceptable scorecard provides the information necessary for negotiation. The initial use of the scorecard is to determine the minimum acceptable score, which in this example was a score of 81. In the example, corporation XYZ scored an 85, which exceeds the minimum by 4 points.

The score card illustrates two features that we believe to be of paramount importance in grading. First, you can see that the XYZ Corporation did not receive a passing grade in priority two, Financial Return (to be discussed

Figure 6
**ACCEPTABLE MULTIPLE PERFORMANCE SCORECARD,
CORPORATION XYZ**

Priority	Description	Weight	Minimum Acceptable	Actual Score	Comments
1	Service Improvement Record	40	36	38	Excellent
2	Financial Return	25	20	17	Offer only $35,000, Need $40,000 minimum
3	Customer Satisfaction	20	15	18	Look to make percentage of fee contingent upon customer surveys
4	Professional Experience	10	7	8	Seek greater role in selection of future managers

later). Any such unacceptable score within an otherwise acceptable proposal typically becomes an item for future negotiation. Second, notice that the acceptable ranges change for every priority. The highest priority has the smallest acceptable range. The top priority (service improvement record) requires a score of 36 (or 90 percent) of the maximum is required while a 20 (or only 80 percent of maximum) is required of priority two. These ranges for acceptable variance expand to 75 percent for priority three; 70 percent for priority four; and 60 percent for priority five.

Lesson 60

The more important the selection criteria is to you, the less acceptable any variance from the maximum score.

If the acceptable multiple performance scorecard shown in the illustration were your actual negotiation position, you would need to communicate this financial shortcoming to your negotiator. As attractive as the offer is, it does not meet your minimum expectation in terms of financial return. You have most likely determined this to be a show stopper, and the deal will not be consummated unless you receive an improved financial return during negotiations. There may be other improvements that you would like to gain through negotiations, but your highest priority and your focus must be to eliminate the shortcoming in priority two. Resolving this issue may very well require a compromise on your part in some other facet of the proposal. You need to determine what you are willing to give up to attain your minimum financial return requirement. The AMPS scorecard provides a nice snapshot of where you may have some wiggle room.

---------------------------------**Lesson 61**-----------------------

When you enter the negotiating stage with your potential partner(s), you must know whether you already have an acceptable offer or still need to gain something beyond the existing proposal. You must distinguish a show stopper from desired items that would simply sweeten the deal. Negotiate hard, but know the difference!

Win-Win Negotiating Strategies

Some individuals use their position of advantage as a power play to force compromise from the other party in face-to-face negotiations. You should use this style only with extreme caution and a complete knowledge of the consequences. These are service negotiations, not labor-management contract disputes. This is a voluntary partnership, and an in-your-face style of negotiation is a questionable approach. You can assume that for most issues there will be information or a competitive advantage held by one party or the other. Likewise, you can be assured that for every point of advantage you have, the prospective partner will have another. You must decide early what style of negotiating you wish to establish.

We strongly recommend that you initially negotiate with more than one, but no more than three, offerors in your early competitive negotiations. Even if you have a clear cut favorite, proceeding through the initial phase of negotiations with more than one offeror keeps your options open. The first stage of the negotiation process should be your formal discussion with each attractive offeror for its best and final offer.

This discussion between the institution and the offeror is an individualized conversation with each of the offerors. Your communications should be clear and concise, and your focus should be on the perceived weaknesses of each offer. Whether you formally advise each offeror of the remaining competitors still under consideration is an institutional decision. Our only advice is that you should only officially advise the firms of this information if you are certain you will award the contract to one of them or not at all. If you are considering awarding the contract to a firm that missed the cut, you should avoid any official announcement to the selected-for-negotiation firms.

Lesson 62

When you seek best and final offers from your potential partners, you are being perceived as interested but not yet committed. Therefore, be specific and direct in your communication. Take your time! Be clear and then give adequate response time.

Lesson 63

As you attempt to close the deal, commit each and every agreement to writing. Be sure that both parties sign each agreement as you proceed through your negotiations. When negotiations are concluded, you both will have authored the best and final offer.

During negotiations always be prepared to discuss alternatives in your efforts to reach a win-win situation. Be careful not to diminish the attractiveness of the offeror. Just as you understood how you want to maximize your organizational strengths, you must not lose sight of the strengths that you must import into your operation from the offeror.

Lesson 64

Negotiations should not involve an attempt to realign the backbone of your prospective partner. Don't lose the strength of their diverse perspective by trying to bludgeon them into submission. Diversity drives.

You need to have both partners emerge from these negotiations as accomplices, not antagonists. If neither party feels that it got everything that it wanted but it is still excited about the venture, you probably have done a great job of negotiating a strong platform for an effective partnership.

Lesson 65

During these negotiations you are establishing the type relationship that you can expect long term from the partnership. The foundation is being set in place; organizational and personal relationships are being developed. You are setting the stone in place!

Dance Partners

Once you have received the best and final responses, the RFP evaluation team has one last scoring task. You have taken a tug at the rope, and if there was any slack in the line the offerors have let you stretch the offer to the limit. Score the responses, and select the firm with which you want to enter into actual contract negotiations. Depending on the policies of your organization, approval to enter into final contract negotiations is often a staff recommendation requiring senior management review and approval. At GMU, senior management often is engaged earlier at the selection of firms to advance to best and final offer stage of negotiations. Our evaluation team usually does not have the authority to advance to the contract negotiation stage without senior management review and approval. Since no step (not even an internal one) should be taken for granted, the team must assume that they will need to sell this contract award recommendation to the senior management of the university. Don't lose the catch lifting the fish into the boat! Once convinced of the wisdom of the decision, the senior management of both entities must remind their legal staff that for all intents and purposes, the deal is done. The message to the attorneys should be straightforward to make sure the legal paperwork is drafted in a binding and professionally acceptable manner.

Since you have engaged your procurement and legal staff throughout the outsourcing process, negotiating the actual legal wording should not be a problem. Famous last words! Stay close to your legal advisors. You can lose a great partnership at this step if the attorneys lose sight of the bigger picture.

Lesson 66

From the beginning of the search process to the end, there is no substitute for preparation, preparation, and preparation! Don't drop the ball! Prep the team on closing the deal!

Early Years of the Partnership

Once you are up and running, you must understand the bottom-line details of the contract. For instance, with a low profit margin service contract, an institution must know and be sensitive to the slim fast profitability of the contract. Concurrent with GMU's decision to outsource mail services came the need for restructuring our retail operation and our residential student mail system. This involved a capital investment in the procurement of new centrally located student mailboxes. Previously, the mailboxes were located in the dormitories. This procurement should have been identified earlier and negotiated as part of the contract, but it wasn't. The outcome of this oversight was that when the contractor was asked to purchase 1,300 mailboxes for $50,000, he balked and insisted that the cost should be borne by the university. Since we fully understood how tight this contract was financially, we agreed to reimburse the contractor through calculated savings over a four-year period resulting from a reduction of labor costs. We would then reimburse the contractor for the installation charge over a four-year period from mailbox rentals. A final piece of the negotiation was that GMU also provided the contractor with a cargo truck including all necessary maintenance, gas, and insurance. The monthly value of this asset was then applied over the remainder of the contract as an offset to the total mailbox purchase price. Sound complicated? It was, but it could have been avoided. We ended up wheeling and dealing with our corporate partner as a result of our request for an additional investment from a firm that we knew had only a nominal profit margin in this venture. Although the responsibility for incurring the capital expenditure was not specified in the contract, our knowledge of the low profit margin did allow us to arrive at a timely and mutually acceptable resolution. The lesson? Know your contract! Sometimes, the only blood that you will squeeze out of a turnip will be your own!

Lesson 67

Hone your negotiating skills often and early! A competitive negotiation mindset begins with the development of the request for proposals. It is simply consummated with the signing of the actual agreement. Negotiations will unquestionably continue throughout the duration of the term of the contract.

Industry Volatility—Contract Length

Don't assume that you will be able to reach an improved understanding with your prospective partner after you sign the contract. If you can't reach mutually satisfying agreements during the negotiation process, it will be an uphill battle during the subsequent term of the contract. In a memorandum of understanding that was attached to our most recent travel contract, it was agreed that any significant change in revenue due to factors beyond the control of either party would constitute grounds for a renegotiation of the financial terms of the contract. This language was possible and essential because both parties understood the volatility of the travel industry. Reaching this agreement early in the process laid the foundation for us to amicably work out all the other terms of a contract. A contract in an industry that is undergoing substantial changes requires continuous evaluation and reassessment. In these types of situations, we have been reluctant to commit to any initial contract term in excess of two years. To balance the needs of our corporate partners, we would typically incorporate language authorizing two or three one-year extension options.

Lesson 68

The contract must address how unforeseen changes beyond the control of either party will be handled and what the responsibility of each party will be.

A Closed Chapter—A New Beginning

The contract award should be treated as a statement of your resolve to achieve the support service mission through the partnership. You must be committed to integrating the corporate partner into the university, and you must be confident you can attain college or university acceptance of the outsourcing venture. For example, in our custodial service contract awards, the occupant customers were informed of the levels and frequencies of services being contracted on their behalf. We have found that our outsourcing success ratio is substantially diminished if we do not share with university staff what services they should expect as a result of the agreement with the contractor. With events management, the real benefit to GMU has been that we integrated the external firm into the fabric of the university community. To this day, most GMU staff members are totally unaware that event management is provided by an outside corporation. Even the corporate staff are believed to be GMU staff. Internal customers just saw a different individual, and there was no change in the organizational structure.

Lesson 69

If your personnel accept the staff of the partner as part of your organization's family, the larger organization will do so as well. This will not usually happen naturally.

When changing the way a service is provided, you must anticipate a less-than-smooth transition. This is not much different than the trauma that often surrounds a transition to a new financial software program package or the introduction of a new employee to a key staff position. The additional complicating feature in a support service change is the introduction of external-to-campus players. The combination of a not-so-accommodating departing party and an eager-to-impress incoming party makes this a tricky hand-off at best. Stay close to the activity during this period, because most fatalities occur at our busiest intersections. Beware of road rage.

Lesson 70

The signing of the contract is often both the beginning and the end. You must be clear in communicating the responsibilities of the outgoing and the incoming parties. The jilted partner can do irreversible harm if you do not treat them as you would want to be treated after losing a contract. Address transition issues in the language of each contract to avoid having to grapple with transition-related negotiations at the conclusion of a contract term.

Part II

The Five-Step Unit Review Process and the High-Five Approach to Blended Management

To apply what was discussed in Part I, this part of the book provides a "Five-Step Unit Review Process" in combination with the "High-Five Approach to Blended Management." This methodology suggests that perhaps you can avoid spending valuable time up front in improving services that are unrelated to your institution's highest priorities.

4

Introduction to the Five-Step Process

THE FIVE-STEP UNIT REVIEW PROCESS	
Step	**Function/Activity**
1	Identify Universe
2	Determine Rationale
3	Evaluate Performance
4	Map/Scan Environment
5	Select the Route

The five-step unit review process is a fully integrated, information driven process designed to give you your best chance of hitting your best practice target. The process consists of the steps listed below, each of which will be described in full in the five chapters that follow.

When proceeding with the five-step process, a detour in a direction that is not supported by the information gathered by the unit review team will typically not be acceptable to the other participants in the process. The built-in conscience of the process lies in the players themselves. The capacity for a team leader, or senior administrator, to impose upon the team a direction that is totally inconsistent with the information gathered has been nearly eliminated. Once this functional unit review has been initiated, the openness of the search for excellence will demand information-driven decision making and those involved will accept nothing less.

Another attractive aspect of the five-step process is that it forces the integration of meaningful information. The process quickly discards frivolous, unrelated information, and focuses its attention on important (often overlooked) interlacing relationships between support services. There is a rigorous review of the importance of these relationships and an identification of how and when they must mesh together to provide a universe of effective support services. The five-step process helps us understand that when one of our support services begins missing the target, there will be a ripple effect throughout our support services universe. Furthermore, the review process enables us to better understand these inter-service relationships so we can better predict the most likely consequences of our decisions prior to actually having to learn every lesson the hard way.

------------------------------ **Lesson 72** ---------------------

Sometimes a best practice is simply letting someone else get the first black eye. We cannot afford to always be the first one to enter the fray. We must pick our spots judiciously!

The five-step unit review process provides assurance that the ultimate decision made on the best approach for a best practice will be based upon solid information—not anecdotes and unfounded rumors. That confidence will reside not only in you and your staff, but will resound throughout your campus community. The reward for your willingness to objectively search for a better way to do things, is that you have opened the eyes of the campus community. They now have a real-life example and can now decide for themselves if a similar journey for excellence is worth the time and effort required. Most importantly, you have left behind your footprints—not necessarily to be blindly followed, but certainly to be used for guidance and direction. You have removed some of the organization's fears and anxieties about change, uncertainty, and chaos.

The five-step approach to best practices may not be your guarantee to a bulls-eye, but it should ensure that you have followed a process that has been complete, comprehensive and, most importantly, totally objective. The greatest value of this approach is the forced integration of related services. The approach forces the institution to discover, evaluate, and improve upon the interrelationships between support service providers. Additionally, there is no way to complete the five-step-approach and avoid serious institutional dialogue concerning the consequences and impacts of every subsequent service delivery decision upon every other support service provider throughout the campus.

A heightened campus awareness of not only the interlacing relationship between the myriad service providers on your campus but also an increased understanding of the importance of the timely and effective delivery of each of these services upon the ultimate quality of the entire institution is an unavoidable by-product of this five-step search process for support service best practices. Our recommended approach has the added bonus of being totally information-driven. When searching for best practices it is often easier to compromise to a less controversial, more consensual path to follow than to follow where the facts actually take you.

Before You Begin: Define Your Priorities

The first three steps in the process will be fairly self-explanatory once you read the next three chapters. But a warning is necessary before you embark on Steps 4 and 5: a college or university must determine the institutional priority of each support service relative to the development of a service improvement plan before beginning Steps 4 and 5. In other words, in the overall priorities of the institution—regardless of the particular evaluation given any specific support service—you need to find out what kind of priority improving this particular support service will have in the bigger picture for advancement of the college or university.

Although it is not one of the five steps, this institutional priority matching process is crucial. By focusing on those support services that will most likely impact the success or failure of your institution's high priority initiatives, you can avoid spending valuable time up front in improving services that are unrelated to your institution's highest priorities.

Lesson 73

Identify the support services that affect your institutional priorities to avoid the risk of pursuing process improvement reviews with no relation to the major priorities of your organization.

At GMU, we use the analogy of a mountain climbing expedition to illustrate the major differences between the first three steps and the last two steps of the five-step process. When we begin the expedition, all support services are identified as part of the team of climbers. All support services continue through determining rationale (Step 2) and evaluating service effectiveness (Step 3). All identified support services at your institution will be identified, rationalized, and evaluated. At this point we will set up our base camp of operations, and we call it Camp Context.

Based on the relationship of each support service to the priorities of the institution, we must determine which service will be the first group to leave Camp Context and climb toward the summit—the development of a best practice.

No institution has the resources to send all teams up the mountain at one time, nor can any institution withstand the risk associated with such a venture. Therefore, we develop a strategy to send up the highest priority support service teams and each team regularly and routinely communicates back to the home base what it has learned.

Priority Plotting

When we have completed our first three steps of the five-step unit review process, and before we embark on the best practice journey, we have found the development of a support service scattergram to be of invaluable assistance. In this analysis, we consider three variables.

- Mission-centrality (or institutional importance)
- Performance effectiveness of the support service
- Resource allocation (time and effort) dedicated to the specific support service.

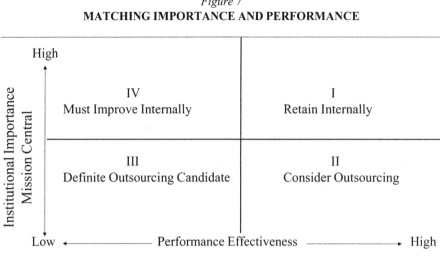

Figure 7
MATCHING IMPORTANCE AND PERFORMANCE

We initially divide the world of support services into the four quadrants shown in figure 7, and only plot the first two variables: mission centrality and service performance effectiveness. In general, those services that are placed in Quadrant I are a pretty healthy match. A Quadrant I plot indicates that we are performing effectively in a support service that is regarded as central to the institution's mission. Those services falling in Quadrant II probably need to be reviewed in terms of the effort/resources being expended since our performance is strong but in a service of low importance to the institution. For services plotted in Quadrant III there is a need to reassess the allocation of any resources. In essence, we have to ask ourselves, why bother?

Finally, a service plotted in Quadrant IV needs an immediate overhaul. The support service is central to the mission of the university, and we are performing poorly. This graph provides a good start towards the establishment of a service priority list for the subsequent best practice search process. However, since we are looking for best practices we can only complete our analysis by superimposing the third variable—a circle of time and effort. This is illustrated in figure 8.

It is essential to determine the resources (time and effort) being expended on each of the support services. Each institution can devise its own definition of low and high levels of effort, but the distinction is of paramount importance when determining which services are in greatest need of near-

Figure 8
PERFORMANCE EFFECTIVENESS

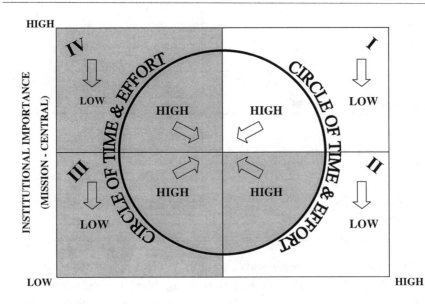

term improvement. Occasionally, a service-miss on either performance or mission relevance can be overlooked if we are only making a nominal time and effort commitment.

The shaded areas in figure 8 are in need of priority attention. The organization's priorities in terms of taking corrective action should be as shown in figure 9.

This scattergram based on the plotting of all support services in relation to these three variables should provide you with the necessary institutional context to select the order of your search teams of best practice climbers. The summary table in figure 10 provides an overview of the meanings associated with each quadrant.

All support services will routinely and regularly make the best practice climb through Steps 4 and 5. As mentioned earlier, those services linked to high priorities of the institution will make the

Figure 9
PRIORITIES

Priority	Location
1.	IV–HIGH
2.	IV–LOW
3.	III–HIGH
4.	III–LOW
5.	II–HIGH
6.	II–LOW
7.	I–HIGH
8.	I–LOW

Figure 10
SUMMARY TABLE

Mission Quadrant	T & E Circle	Summary Evaluation
I	HIGH	Good return on investment . . . maybe some tinkering?
I	LOW	Possibly an institutional best practice.
II	HIGH	Poor return, consider restructuring, delivery change.
II	LOW	Look for lessons learned, portability, delivery change.
III	HIGH	A disaster! Outa here—close shop!
III	LOW	Serious candidate for reallocation and/or elimination.
IV	HIGH	Circle the wagons; change service management ASAP.
IV	LOW	Consider increased investment or delivery change.

trek first, but those support services not linked to a high institutional priority must also search for best practices. For each institution, it is a question of time and effort as well as an analysis of one's return on investment.

Lesson 74

Expand upon your natural opportunities for rigorous evaluation and incorporate within them this organizational process to search for best practices.

Whether your services are self-operated or outsourced, you should take advantage of already-in-place activities to engage in this continuous approach for improved service quality. There is a strong parallelism between your self-operated services and your contracted services in this search for excellence process. For instance, on no less than an annual basis, you engage in either an employee performance evaluation (for your self-operations) or an annual service evaluation (for your contract services). Use the opportunity to search a little for best practices!

In a slightly more formal manner, services that are already outsourced will complete Steps 4 and 5 of the process when the service contract comes up for renewal or re-award. Keep in mind, however, that the pursuit of best practices will not happen automatically just because you are rebidding an outsourced activity. There will be no search for excellence if you simply readvertise the same RFP or IFB that you used five years ago. The outsourced service only has a chance to bring you a best practice if you commit to routine rigorous environmental scanning. The purpose of this scanning is to find somewhere on the radar screen that blip (in or outside of higher education) that becomes your target, which is your best practice.

This strategy ensures that all your support services regularly and routinely are engaged in the continuous search for best practices. The first climbers are those services determined to be essential to the organization if it is to be effective in achieving its institutional priorities. Time is of an essence for the journey of these climbers. We will learn from their travel experiences and each of the other support service teams will use this information for similar trips at a later time. These search for service excellence trips may be accomplished within functional review processes, RFP-IFB transitions, or specially designed exercises as determined by the organization. The point is that most institutions have in place best practice search opportunities, it is just a matter of taking advantage of existing management chances for strategic service improvement.

5

Step 1: Identify Your Universe of Services

THE FIVE-STEP UNIT REVIEW PROCESS	
Step	**Function/Activity**
1	**Identify Universe**
2	Determine Rationale
3	Evaluate Performance
4	Map/Scan Environment
5	Select the Route

Step 1 in the five-step unit review process is simply taking stock. At GMU, this process began by pulling together a small group of university officials to define support services and then inventory those services. It was a worthy effort, which concluded with a list that was a potpourri of the names of offices and the names of functions or activities.

This list was initially quite shocking to the group, as it totaled more than 100 support services. The members of the review group circulated this list throughout the university for comment and comprehensiveness. As we expected, the inventory of support services list grew even longer as we received feedback from the field. As a general rule, our advice during this exercise is to be sure to err on the side of inclusiveness. If the suggested activity did not really seem to be a support service, we still added it to the support service universe. Being overly inclusive early in this process has no real downside, because several subsequent purging stages are built into the process. It is also essential to include all support services regardless of the source of delivery. The review must include outsourced support services, as well as those provided by university support staff. This inventory review must also occur on a routine and regular basis. We have seen support services added and eliminated over the years as we re-establish the support service universe each year.

The annual review of this inventory is essential. Likewise, it is critical that you engage the broader university in the exercise. Every year we find ourselves adding services to the university that have either emerged over the past 12 months as a new service, were simply missed in our last universe identification process, or now represent a merged service of formerly separate services. Accomplishing universe currency is an essential first step in our search for service excellence.

---------------------**Lesson 75**-----------------------

Every administrative activity is most likely a support service. It is best to err on the side of being over-inclusive when defining the universe of services to engage in functional review process.

Significant institutional learning occurs at this first step of taking an accurate inventory. At this stage, you begin to take notice of the number of support services, the relationship between them, and the ambiguity in the existing names of the offices. Activities that the review group identifies as potentially duplicative, ambiguous, overlapping, or simply confusing should be investigated further for information, verification, and explanation.

Many issues can be resolved at this initial stage, so resist the temptation to skip over this first step of creating an accurate inventory of your universe of support services. At GMU, we discovered several activities identified as distinct and separate simply because they had in the past been given separate budgets or had different sources of funding. This initial stage of purging the inventory allowed us to combine some activities that were providing very similar services, but had been seen as distinct due to their separate accounts. Additionally, we were actually able to immediately initiate some organizational restructuring, because we found one situation where duplicative services were being provided by two offices.

----------------------------**Lesson 76**-------------------

It is not possible to improve process integration, parallel sequencing, or interlacing effectiveness without an accurate inventory of service activities.

We hope your number of surprises at this stage will be minimal. It is always a bit of a shock when a group discovers the existence of an office that it thought had been eliminated or the name of an individual who the group had thought had long since left the employ of the university.

6

Step 2: Determine Rationale for Services

THE FIVE-STEP UNIT REVIEW PROCESS	
Step	**Function/Activity**
1	Identify Universe
2	**Determine Rationale**
3	Evaluate Performance
4	Map/Scan Environment
5	Select the Route

In Step 2 of the process of critical review, the college or university must ask the question, "Why are we providing this service?"

When GMU began this "reason for living" stage of the process, it was probably no different than most colleges universities who see this review of service rationale as an activity with no real need for immediacy. What quickly brought us to a sense of urgency and what we have learned along the way is worth sharing. We had a university mission statement like every other university in the country. The words were so global in nature, it was hard to determine what we were not attempting to accomplish. Any type of support service could easily connect itself somehow to the university mission statement. Until the university tightened its mission statement, there was no apparent need to tighten, or in some cases to even develop, unit mission statements.

Well, this sloppiness changed rather dramatically during the early-to-mid 1990s. In the early 1990s, student housing was experiencing its first decline in popularity. This appeared to be related to an economic downturn in the metropolitan region. All of a sudden families in the immediate area were making quality residential space available for lease, and our downturn in the local real estate economy meant that for the first time in the history of GMU, our students had attractive off campus housing opportunities. This new life-style option, combined with GMU's relatively high on-campus housing prices, resulted in a significant decline in the number of students living on campus. And many of those students that stayed in on-campus housing were less than satisfied with the accommodations, the rules, the mandatory meal plan, the housing staff, and university life in general.

We seemed to lack the internal capacity to reverse the downward occupancy spiral, and having no reasonable mission statement for student housing didn't help the situation. With some assistance from the student housing staff at Georgia Tech (they were engaged in some creative housing partnerships related to the 1996 Summer Olympics being held in Atlanta, Georgia), we developed an RFP to outsource the management and operation of student housing. Some elements (e.g. student discipline, etc.) were retained as the responsibility of the university, but for the most part we were looking to outsource the entire operation. We knew that no other university had taken this path, but we were convinced that if we could change the traditional student housing culture of captive audience to one of guest-innkeeper, we could return to our earlier days of full capacity in the dormitories.

Mission Identity

The eventual decision to outsource was more difficult than we expected, and the transition was much longer than anyone ever anticipated. We had not completed answered the question, "Why student housing at GMU?" We had not engaged in a comprehensive review and dialogue on the relationship between student housing and the mission of the university. With only 3,000 of our more than 25,000 students living on campus, GMU was not primarily residential. Another issue we did not address before we released the RFP was that student housing clearly had an identity crisis. Although we only got a few responses to this 1995 RFP, all of the offerors noted the need to address the centrality of housing to the long-term mission of the university.

This deficiency forced GMU and its corporate partner to engage in mission-related dialogue throughout the early stages of the three year contract. The university has no doubt that the transition would have been much smoother had we been able to include in our original RFP a clear statement of the mission, goals and objectives of student housing in relation to university life.

Mission Congruity

The second bell-ringer for GMU was the 1995–96 construction of the Johnson Center, which is a 300,000 square foot facility in the middle of campus that contains a major library of over 100,000 square feet, and a student union in the remainder of the facility. It was like a feeding frenzy when the newly constructed space was being considered for allocation. The president made it clear, however, that nothing would be housed in the Johnson Center that could not show a clear connection with the teaching and learning mission of the university. Any doubt about the seriousness of this edict was short-lived. Within weeks of hearing about the president's position, the campus community learned that the recreation game room concept with pool tables, air hockey and ping pong, failed this relational test, and had lost its anticipated space in the Johnson Center.

The real lesson here, however, has nothing to do with the space allocation decision-making process at the Johnson Center. Instead, the best practice lesson lies in how the university community came to understand the necessary integration and congruity of departmental, school, college, and university missions. At GMU, the recreational game room did not end up a loser in the process, it simply did not fit the Johnson Center's mission of establishing a pervasive learning environment. The game room continued to be seen as a significant resource in achieving the institutional objective of improving university life on campus and was soon selected for prime space in the newly renovated Student Union Building I facility. The game room has nicely filled a void, and university life has improved as a result.

The university was in the "we'll get to it . . . whenever" mode of developing mission statements for each support service, but these two bell-ringing events spurred departmental mission statement progress. Although the mission statements had little weight in the actual allocation of space in the new facility, as a result of this unit mission exercise, every unit improved its knowledge of the mission of the university, and how it could assist in the attainment of those goals.

Mission Understanding

Identifying the mission and rationale for the existence of a support service is an activity that not only provides rationale for our efforts, but also determines the general acceptance of the service. In other words, we must determine if the greater college or university shares the same opinion about the need for providing the service. The question of institutional priority is important and can only be accomplished through campus-wide discussion. If there is an agreed-upon rationale for the service, you must next determine how important the delivery of this service is to the effective core mission of teaching and learning. The greater the distance a support service is from the core mission of the college or university, the tougher the questions should be relative to institutional resources provided and/or staff energy and time devoted to such support services.

At GMU, we review the rationale of our support services with broad institutional input. We see no lasting value in the development of a service mission statement authored by a unit supervisor, director of auxiliary enterprises, and institutional business manager. Such a rationale review would be inconsistent with our philosophy of blended management, parallel sequencing, and service interlacing. We expand the "reason for being" review team beyond the direct service provider organization, and then seek concurrence from senior management on the rationale and priority of each support service. This provides the institution with a better feel for each of its support services and the impact each has upon core competencies.

Words of Caution

Now that you understand the first two steps in the five-step unit review process, it's time to pause and listen to some words of caution before you proceed with the next three steps. As simple as these first two steps are, we have learned that most institutions do not want to follow a step-by-step instruction manual. Most of us want to blow past the first two steps, roll up our sleeves and start tackling the issue of service improvement. You feel that a particular service is not operating satisfactorily, and you think you know what to do to resolve the matter. We understand why you will be tempted not to follow this step-by-step unit review process: You want to fix something! And you want to fix it now. You are being barraged with anecdotal information and numerous complaints. You are suffering from a lack of reliable, accurate information. However, be wary!

"Think like a man of action, act like a man of thought."

—Henri-Louis Bergson

Our experiences at GMU have proven that what we capture in these first two steps is simply invaluable to us in finding a long-term solution to improved performance.

Lesson 77

There simply is no shortcut around taking the time and making the effort to accurately and comprehensively identify:

It is critical that these three questions be answered before embarking on your real interest, which is how can I do this better. Fixing business process problems is in your comfort zone.

- What are you doing?

- Who (sequencing and interlacing) is engaged in the effort?

- Why you are doing the activity?

You may not have the solution figured out yet, but you know when you are unsatisfied with the performance of a particular support service. But if you avoid the first two steps of the process and fail to answer these three questions, your solution to improve performance will be off target. Your solution won't have a chance to hit the target, because you didn't take the time to understand the relationship between the particular support service and the bigger mission of the university.

Lesson 78

When time is of an essence, hurry but don't rush. Make as few long-range commitments as possible.

To prove our point, we share with you this story about one of our own quick fix disasters. Two years after the actual events occurred, we are just now beginning to see some of the humor that one might associate with the errors of our ways. Maybe it will bring a quick smile to your face, and perhaps it will remind you of one of your institution's own quick fix disasters.

Solutions, Not Shortcuts

We have a really nice restaurant on campus that is run by our food service contractor, which passed the test to have space in the Johnson Center. As those of you responsible for food service on your campus are well aware, any free standing restaurant has great difficulty generating sufficient revenues to match expenditures. Well, we also have an outstanding Center for the Arts, which brings in nationally renowned artists throughout the year. Many of these are evening events, and the patrons are looking for some place to catch dinner before the event. The two responsible directors got together, and it looked like a match made in heaven. It looked like we could achieve additional revenue for the restaurant while increasing the number of well-nourished, satisfied arts patrons.

Maybe it was poor marketing or the wrong dinner course menu. Maybe it was the wrong night of the week or the wrong type of event. But whatever the reason, the number of patrons using the restaurant was abysmal and showed no signs of improving. The quick solution was to reduce the labor costs, and hope that the Arts Center director, who also felt badly about the poor attendance, could better market this fine dining, pre-program option to her patrons in the future. As only Murphy's Law can deliver, the very next event resulted in unprecedented numbers of interested diners, greeted by a significantly downsized restaurant staff. As one would expect, these arts patrons were either unable to get served before the event, or received such slow service that they missed a good portion of the arts production.

Lesson 79

If implementation of the bandage approach is necessary because time is of such an essence, than the post-implementation follow-up sessions to develop an integrated, long-term solution must be scheduled in a similarly timely fashion. That is our organizational promise to each other!

In hindsight, we can see the cause of the problem: neither director took the time to figure out what we were trying to accomplish. After this disaster, an intense functional review began in earnest, and by the beginning of the next season, these two outstanding divisions within the university had established a solid system of inter-division coordination. The system has as its foundation an early-alert reservation system that communicates the number of patrons planning to dine at the university restaurant thereby allowing the restaurant manager to staff accordingly. The system is successful, however, because a) the food service director promised that the restaurant would never be marginally understaffed, and b) the arts center director provided a financial guarantee of a minimum level of business. They both found that they could cope with the uncertainty of numbers if they shared the financial risks of the endeavor. Today they both know much more about each other's business, which allows them to make better decisions for the university. We located our moving target and as a result, we have learned the art of dining.

Bandage Not Bondage Solutions

At George Mason University, we are just as anxious to implement quick fixes as anyone else. So we have integrated a "low hanging fruit" philosophy into our continuous unit/function review culture that mandates the correction of our obvious flaws in as timely a fashion as possible. However, this corrective action comes with a flip-side mandate: before making such a fix, we must identify it as only a bandage solution. Before the bandage solution is implemented, the plan must be announced to all affected parties. This is our acknowledgment that this is a compromise approach to finding the real solution.

Once we have determined that corrective action must be implemented immediately, we know that such action will be unsettling to at least one unit within the university. Not all voices will be heard on a particular matter. Therefore, there is a mandatory responsibility on the party implementing the change to gather the appropriate group together to determine what permanent process improvements, if any, need to be established. This must be accomplished in a timely manner.

Lesson 80

We must dedicate sufficient time and effort to communication if we are to achieve a better understanding of what we are really trying to do and why we are doing it.

We demand this from each other because we realize that quick fix solutions are actions taken without the benefit of either sufficient breadth of input or institutional context. Our "low hanging fruit philosophy" allows us to quickly correct obvious deficiencies in our operations, while still requiring us to give timely context to the issue to determine the best permanent solution to the problem.

7

Step 3: Evaluate Performance of Services

THE FIVE-STEP UNIT REVIEW PROCESS	
Step	**Function/Activity**
1	Identify Universe
2	Determine Rationale
3	**Evaluate Performance**
4	Map/Scan Environment
5	Select the Route

Step 3 in the review process is to establish performance measures for each aspect of every subset of the service universe under review. Over the years, we have found that what is the most important performance measure in one area of food service (board plan) is often not the most important measure in another area (catering) under the support service umbrella of food service. It is important for both parties to understand the performance differences. For example, it would not be unusual to determine that food quality and variety of selection is the most important variable in your board plan aspect of your food service contract. On the other hand, quality of staff, timeliness, and presentation of food may be of greatest importance to you in the catering aspect of your food service contract. These subtle differences must be communicated to your partner. A sure-fire way to make the point is to give greater weight to those service indicators of greatest importance when evaluating the performance of the contractor.

Lesson 81

Contracts encompassing multiple services require multiple grades for performance. Establish specific measures and scores for the performance of each service and subservice included within the contract.

Corporate Measures

We have also found that it is helpful to determine, in services that outsource, how the service-providing firm itself evaluates the contract with the university. Ask yourself the following performance measure questions:

- Why was the private firm interested in your contract in the first place?

- Now that the firm has the contract, how does it evaluate the contract?

- What corporate performance measures are they using relative to your contract?

- Is the firm interested in renewing the contract? If so, why?

These corporate performance measures may not always be readily available from the third party contractor. You should, however, be adamant in your demands to have access to corporate performance measures. As we have become a little smarter about outsourcing, we have started requesting much of this information from our prospective partner before signing the contract.

Lesson 82

Know your partner's performance indicators! Many of their performance indicators will also be yours. They become shared measures of evaluation.

There are two immediate benefits to obtaining the corporate performance indicators. First, it improves your understanding of your partner. This can only enhance the relationship. Second, it will reaffirm the difference between the perspective of the private contractor and the perspective of the college or university. This understanding is healthy, if remembered; mortal if forgotten!

The story of GMU's expansion of the exclusive food service contract illustrates the importance of corporate performance indicators. We know that from our food service contractor's perspective, exclusivity and expansiveness were the ultimate objectives. We understood this, just as you certainly understand why your corporate partners compete for exclusivity on your campus. However, if you provide related-but-separable services and place a high value on the delivery of each service, you must be willing to contract with different companies to provide the related services.

Lesson 83

Your search for specific best practices in separate services must expand beyond the corporate organizational parameters of your private industry or public organization.

When contracting for food service in the recent past, we have shown a willingness to contract with separate firms for vending, catering, convenience store, restaurant and pub, and food court kiosks. In recent RFPs, we actually included language that encourages vendors and firms to bid on specific pieces of a larger support service. We refer to this as modular outsourcing. We have learned several lessons in our efforts to link service-specific performance with our provider selection process:

Lesson 84

Without service-specific performance evaluations, there is no way to determine which services are performing unsatisfactorily for the consideration of your service provider(s).

Lesson 85

Corporate partners strong in performance in one activity are not necessarily strong in all of the other contract-required services desired by the college or university.

Lesson 86

Multiple vendor selection may be the best choice for the college or university, but such a choice will always increase the institution's contract administration activity (read: increased coordination responsibilities).

As important as it is to establish these specific sub-service performance measures, it is equally critical that these be developed in a consensus building manner. If the service is currently being outsourced, your partner must fully understand the criteria for evaluation. Likewise, if the service is a university operated service, these criteria must be routinely communicated throughout the organization and evaluated on a regular basis. We often underestimate the need for the broader organization to understand the evaluation criteria for some of our support services. For example, you might be amazed by the contributions that can be made by tenured faculty in biotechnology toward improving your mail delivery service, if you just let them know what you are trying to achieve.

Lesson 87

The key element of evaluating support service performance is outcome analysis. You must baseline current benefits and specify future expectations.

Financial Performance Analysis

Establishing financial performance measures is no easy task, and it is essential that baseline financial performance data be developed. This most likely can be initiated at the field level of the service organization. It cannot be completed at the field level, however, because most universities require that management establish an institutional cost-benefit policy. We must adopt in total, or some hybrid of, the concept of responsibility center budgeting. Such a policy adoption is consistent with our commitment to look at the whole picture, not simply what is easily visible. The identification of indirect costs, as well as the more obvious direct costs, is critical to any scheme of financial performance evaluation.

You must keep in mind that establishing the financial base line data is by definition an exercise in compromise. Each university must determine for itself what level of sophistication in number crunching is satisfactory for future decision making. Your accountants can provide endless numbers of financial calculations to refine the development of your baseline cost benefit analysis. To its absolute extreme, every expense made in every university support service can be collapsed into the program of instruction. It is then even possible to collapse all college and school expenditures into learning.

You must ask yourself during this cost accounting refinement . . . for what purpose?

Lesson 88

Your task here is not an easy one, because you must determine what financial information you need for accurate performance evaluation and good decision making. You need the right stuff!

Broad Breadth Evaluations

Once the evaluation is completed and the support service area is determined to be an institutional priority, it is time for the college or university to begin the search for support service best practices. A key reminder is that you are focusing on services that directly impact the highest priorities of the institution. You are selecting these support services because you are looking for the greatest return on the investment of resources. You must avoid having a support service become a show-stopper as your institution attacks a high priority initiative. You will expend the greatest amount of time and effort on those support services with the closest linkage to your institutional priorities. Obviously, the lower the evaluation grade for any of these services the greater the required effort. You will be giving the greatest priority to those services closely linkage to your institutional priorities and receiving less than satisfactory grades. Get your support services clear of all dangerous intersections!

You must ensure that your support services are totally integrated within the academic mission of the university. Once your support services realize they are responsible for providing support to achieve the core values of the institution, you have indeed left the ledge and begun the leap of faith. You won't know upon which particular support service to focus your attention to improve high quality admission yields and retention rates unless you have already taken the time to identify the support services that you provide (Step 1), determine why they are being provided (Step 2), and evaluate how well they are being provided (Step 3).

Equipped with that information, you become a valuable asset to your college or university in its quest to attain its academic and campus life objectives. Collectively, personnel from support services, academic affairs, and university life can now strategize to determine what activities and/or functions appear to be most determinative of success/failure in either attracting better students or improving retention. The beauty of what you are now bringing to the decision-making table is that you know the kind of information necessary, and the action to be taken, to attain the academic objectives of the institution. Without the time and effort that you have given to the support service unit review, support service decisions to enhance the retention of high quality students would have been based upon a gut feeling rather than being information driven. It must be inescapably evident that this support service review information (what and why the different services impact retention, and then how well the support service is being provided) is simply invaluable in any decision making process to achieve greater retention. You need only ask yourself how many times you were in dire straits because you were being forced to make a decision without that kind of relational information. With the right information you can make the right decision.

Functional Review Team

Reviewing the performance of existing support services is easier now that the support services have all been identified, interrelationships have been uncovered and the rationale for the existence of each support service has been determined. There is no boilerplate matrix for performance measures, but it is essential that the institution develop a set of qualitative and quantitative performance measures for each of its support services. If the service has been outsourced to a third party there should be a direct relationship between these performance measures and the language of your RFP. On the other hand, if university staff manages the operation, there should be a strong linkage between the performance measures and the job description of the staff providing the service. Performance measures are developed through both top-down and bottom-up input, as well as industry specific benchmarking information.

Institutions must remember that if a particular aspect of a service is important, the university must regularly remind the provider of its importance, and then the institution must aggressively evaluate this feature of the service. The service will not improve if it is not evaluated. Additionally, an over-generalized service evaluation, where specific service standards are critical, will be frustrating to both the provider and the institution. Leave nothing to doubt.

An example of the importance of performance review is an experience we recently had with our food services. Our outsourced food service partner provides food service for our student board plan, a bistro, a restaurant, a food court in the Johnson Center, another food outlet in the student union, as well as all of our catering on campus. Each of these food outlets is very important. One general overall annual evaluation of food service would simply not be productive. If five of the six areas receive a grade of excellence, but the sixth area is graded poorly, the average grade might be good to very good. If the poor grade, however, was in an area of great importance, the partnership may be about to come to an abrupt end, which under an over-generalized evaluation would come as a total surprise to your private contractor.

---------------------- **Lesson 89** ----------------------

Improve communications. Reduce assumptions of shared perspective.

We have just begun to embark on our long journey for continued improvement. We hope you picked up some helpful hints and necessary supplies here. Our quest for excellence continues!

8

Step 4: Mapping and Scanning the Environment

THE FIVE-STEP UNIT REVIEW PROCESS	
Step	**Function/Activity**
1	Identify Universe
2	Determine Rationale
3	Evaluate Performance
4	**Map/Scan Environment**
5	Select the Route

At George Mason University, Step 4—the actual mapping and scanning for best practices—is the fun phase of the process. It has not always been this way, but today this process seems to have become a way of life for staff. Although there never seems to be enough time in the day to dedicate to scanning, you must find the time. Smart organizations only become smart and stay that way by providing an encouraging environment to allow their people to work smartly. As an institution, we are slowly getting over the natural defensive retort, "I don't have time to reflect on what we are trying to do because I am too busy just trying not to fall further and further behind." We must remind ourselves that these kinds of natural responses will come from not only our average and weaker staff personnel, but also from some of our best and most effective staffers. So this is not a time to kill the messenger!

Unit Review Teams

This is the time to assess who your most effective leaders will be in identifying potential best practices. The most effective way to attack this assignment is to select a team of individuals with a bulldog mentality for digging in the details, and a collective capacity to bring out the best thinking from each member of the team. Remember that you need to include creative thinkers, and outside-of-the box pioneers. Do not underestimate the importance of your selections. Remind yourself of the time and effort that you have already invested in this process. Your selection of team members will either expand the horizons of possible improvement beyond what was ever thought possible, or they will become the debilitating variable that will limit your range of improvements to mere incrementalism. You will have every possible type of personnel issue associated with your selection of this team. For instance, you may decide not to place a service manager on the process improvement team, while a subordinate may be placed on the team. Someone from another division may be put on the team, while someone within the division being evaluated may not be part of the team. You will put outsiders to the university on the team, while knowledgeable insiders will be left off. Remember, this ain't no beauty contest!

The selection of the members of this team is critical because they have to find the potential best practices. There is no blueprint for team selection success, but there is some guidance that will serve you well. First and foremost, you must select your best and brightest. Don't put Mr. John Smith on the team simply because he has been the manager of the support service division for the past 20 years. You will likely have a communication issue with him as a result of your decision to exclude him, but it just means addressing this as you would any other sensitive personnel matter. Sometimes it can be as straightforward as advising him of the institutional need to retain his steady and stable direction of the actual operation during this improvement plan stage of the unit review.

----------------------------- **Lesson 90** -----------------------------

Do not defer decisions on personnel-related issues because of ongoing unit review activities.

Having said that, you simply cannot afford to compromise your selectivity criteria for team membership.

Lesson 91

Do not lower the potential of the team by including individuals on the best practice unit review team because you prefer not to deal with pending unresolved employee personnel related problems.

Limit the team to value added personnel. The mistake that we often make is thinking that value added means experience in the particular support service being reviewed. That really is not the case. Although it is imperative that the team be represented with expertise in the service area, it is equally important that the team represent out-of-the-box thinkers, as well as upstream and down-stream affected parties. Almost every best practice search team we have created has also had a current student on the team. The perspective of students is almost always lost when they are not active members of the team. You need to get the student perspective straight from the student. Do not assume that you are getting a student perspective by placing a member of your student services staff on the team. For the most part, these different types of perspectives can be found within your own organization. Not always, however! On several occasions, we have determined that our breadth of collective experience and available critical thinking would most likely result in us only being able to make an incremental improvement. We added outside help.

Lesson 92

If a unit review team comprised exclusively of the internal staff of the organization will not take you to your desired level of performance, you must add the necessary quantity and quality of external representation.

It has also been helpful for us to include individuals who have a history of being critical of the support service. Two recent examples that have really fortified our belief in the advantage of this strategy have been in the selection of alternative delivery systems for mail services and travel services. In both of these processes, the participation of the campus critic has been invaluable to our attainment of improved service performance. In the travel process, the input of this individual persuaded the group that a best practice did not really require greater diversity of choice of travel agency, but simply one firm fully dedicated to high priority service. As a team, we could have easily missed this subtlety since the complaints seemed more related to freedom of choice than to one-stop shopping. In our search for a best practice it became clear that the conceptual driver for improvement was the establishment of dedicated travel management expertise on campus. That clarity of purpose was critical in the subsequent alternative delivery evaluation stage.

In the mail service deliberations, the university critics were able to focus the best practice search group on the only two factors (accuracy and timeliness) that were of any real concern to the university community. One of the key by-products that we gained from their involvement on the team is the expanded knowledge base throughout the institution. While the mail service staff was most concerned about operational issues, (mail-stop numbers, number of campus deliveries, level of staffing, vehicles for multiple campus deliveries, etc.) other non-mail group members explained that all the university really expected from the mail service was timely and accurate delivery of the mail. Those who had been amongst the most critical of the service are now much more understanding of the complexity and commitment of the staff members actually providing the mail service. Spread the good word!

Environmental Scanning, Not Selection

Although the reluctance to go outside the organization to look for assistance in the search for a best practice is understandable, we must avoid reinventing the wheel every time we look for best practices. With the quick and easy access through the Internet, our staffs can be exchanging best practice information and ideas with some of the best institutions in the country.

The most difficult thing to accomplish at this stage of identifying best practices is to keep the search 99.44 percent Ivory soap pure. The purpose of the search is to identify any potential best practices currently being provided in a more efficient and effective service. Warning! The members on the team will either consciously or unconsciously want the plan to bleed into the alternative delivery system selection stage. You must monitor their efforts in such a manner to avoid this bleeding. For example, if you are to sight a best practice photo duplicating operation at Pennsylvania State University, you must remind the team that it is the service that has been determined a best practice—not necessarily the service provided. The reviewing and then selection of the most appropriate delivery system at your institution is determined at Step 5. There is no advantage to bleeding too early. Allowing the process to prematurely advance into that next stage at this time will unnecessarily escalate the anxiety of all those staff that may be affected by any future change in the system of service delivery.

If the established culture of your university is one of daily, continuous improvement, and this is an ongoing part of the duties and responsibilities of the entire staff, the search for best practices will not be nearly as threatening to the existing service support staff. The key to the successful completion of this step is institutional preparedness and open organizational communications. All individuals even remotely involved in this support service under review should at this stage of the process have a much better understanding of the objective of the exercise. The culture of continuous improvement, even if it was totally absent on your campus prior to initiating this support service review process, should be something that you can build upon by this time in the process. If all the previous steps of the process were as open and honest as suggested, your staff will be eager to accept the new challenges associated with positive change.

This service improvement process is not about preparing the university for outsourcing. If you are proceeding through this environmental scanning stage solely as a justification for outsourcing delivery, stop! Just skip this step. As much as we submit that you are grossly mistaken to have made such a decision prior to the mapping and scanning of the environment, do not belabor the process by a time-consuming effort here by some of your best staff. If you have already made the decision to change your future delivery system, it will be obvious to everyone. Do not abuse and misuse your staff at this stage, simply to obtain a blueprint for success to be given to another service provider. Keeping the process pure is your responsibility, as well as the responsibility of the team.

It will be a shame if you do jump the gun here because there is so much for you to learn during this fourth step of out-of-the-box searching for best practices. Not only will you discover how to really ratchet up your service, but you will discover a great deal more about the strengths of your service staff. You will be able to determine whether they can take you to the next level, and you will discover the types of tools that you will need to provide them to be successful. You will also gain the information necessary to be able to more accurately weigh the advantages and disadvantages associated with any change in delivery systems. It has become clear to us that the decision on changing or retaining service delivery systems is much simpler once we have completed the first four steps of the process. Therefore, we strongly recommend that you complete an exhaustive mapping and scanning for best practices prior to making the selection of an alternative delivery system. Time is on your side now. Time becomes more critical when you enter the analysis and selection phase or what we refer to as the fifth element.

Broad-based Scanning

The other lesson learned in doing these best practice searches is that of service integration. No service is an island! Therefore, it is highly unlikely that a service plan can be developed without significant engagement of other service areas. You may even determine that the relationship between two service areas is so strong that environmental scanning for one best practice search cannot be achieved without being pursued in concert with a best practice for the related support service. Never reject an obvious need to expand the search process to include other critical, integrated processes! You may have discovered a tangential support service that has an overlapping but overlooked relationship with the support service under review. There could be gold in those hills!

One fairly recent example of such a service inter-relationship at GMU has been the identification of a significant overlap between our credit union service contract and our banking service contract. What were two unrelated entities in the 1980s, are now two services where any change by one directly impacts the other. The knowledge of this increased overlap and potential friction between the two industries has alerted us to the need to have both parties involved when one of the two is recommending a change in service. We learned this lesson the hard way when we began to accommodate a request from one of the service providers to provide a student mailing list for the purpose of offering a service that we were unaware they provided, but for which the other contractor believed he had an exclusive contract to provide. One effort on our part to communicate and coordinate with both these service providers about the proposal would have allowed us to avoid a very difficult confrontation.

────────────────── ▐ **Lesson 93** ▌ ──────────────────
Potentially inefficient and/or overlapping services can better serve
and accommodate the needs of our customers in a non-duplicative
manner when we develop regular, timely systems of open communication to navigate and negotiate effective means to eliminate cus-
tomer-perceived inefficiencies and inconveniences.
──

External Scanning Support

An example of the need to bring in external expertise to a best practice
search team to help us define irregular interrelationships has been in our
review of print services. As the university has developed multiple campuses
in Fairfax, Arlington, and Prince William counties, it was clear that we
needed a print service master plan to support these three geographically separate campuses (15 miles apart). The technology was changing so rapidly, we
determined that it was essential to bring in our on-campus corporate partner to
assist us in defining some of the more important changes in the document
management industry. The corporate staff understood that their involvement
would neither assist, nor hinder, their future opportunities in providing their
product or service to GMU. The group understood that the discussion was
limited to the future direction of the industry, and its ramification upon print
services at GMU. This sharing of ideas without reference to brand name products or services was only possible because the two parties had established a
solid business relationship based upon trust and understanding. If there was
ever any doubt about the wisdom of requesting this corporate assistance, it
totally dissipated at the first team meeting when the corporate attendees were
management analysts rather than corporate sales personnel.

Although we are still in the midst of approving our print service master
plan, the input from these corporate consultants has already been invaluable.
In the very first meeting, they were able to objectively share with us their perspective that the biggest obstacle to institutional improvement in document
imaging, print services, publications, or document management is usually the
organization's own problems of territoriality between the print service staff
and computing staff. The corporate consultants only had to make the point
once before it became perfectly clear to us that the conceptual driver of print
services in the 21st century was going to be technology, and we knew that
these two university offices had not yet reached the point of totally effective

interaction. Who knows how much time we would have wasted before zeroing in on this university organizational problem without the perceptive insight of the corporate consultants? Bulls-eye!

Lesson 94

The great opportunity for improved effectiveness is not in the emerging of technology (support services), but in the merging of technologies (support services).

We have subsequently been able to bring these two staffs much more closely together on this search for best practice print services. Although we may need to go back to private industry for additional assistance before finalizing our master plan, we will have a much better understanding of: where we are today; what issues and obstacles we are confronting; and where we are heading. This improved institutional understanding is directly attributable to our willingness to listen to the experts in the field. Now, if we decide to consider outsourcing, we are in a position to have the corporate service providers affirm our plan rather than give us a first grade instruction. This integration of internal/external staff on this service improvement plan also will give the university much greater confidence in its collective ability to make wise decisions in this quickly changing service area. Why would anyone ever skip over this step of environmental scanning and mapping?

Scanning Sensitivity

Sharing is caring! The process of searching for best practice support services is a tough love kind of exercise. If done correctly, participants really take part ownership in the operation, and you can never have enough people wanting to assume some responsibility for the success of the support service activities. Therefore, the last action within this scanning step is sharing the findings with the appropriate personnel within the organization. If we follow the process correctly:

- We will identify best practices through broad participation;
- We will identify the interrelationships between this service and other activities;
- We will predict the intended outcomes; and

- We will integrate the insights from both the internal detractors and the external experts.

We should feel pretty confident that this sighting of potential best practices represents solid examples of possible courses of action for improvement. It is time to float the boats!

Do not avoid the chance to get additional input at this stage. We have found that an institutional, open-forum, town meeting opportunity works incredibly well. The great misconception here, which is often held by members of the service improvement team, is that someone in the greater university community is lurking in the bushes just waiting for the chance to scuttle the preliminary findings of the best practice search mission. This is not going to happen; not in a million years!

Nothing but good things will come to you as a result of this moment of northern exposure. This open forum event guarantees you increased knowledge and understanding throughout the campus. You are more-than-prepared to respond to any unenlightened critic or cynic. You and your team are so well prepared that any valid recommended refinement or suggestion from the floor will register with you immediately and you will be able to graciously show your appreciation for the suggestion, your understanding of the potential advantages and disadvantages of the modification, and your willingness to consider its incorporation. This institution-wide opportunity for greater input is the icing on the cake!

---------------------------------**Lesson 95**------------------------------

The search for best practices must reflect the priorities of the greater college or university. As institutional objectives change, so will the need for improving the performance of certain support services. Understanding context is essential!

Environmental Scanning Context

A quick example of the necessity of this step of understanding organizational context, and identifying your universe, is the World Congress on Information Technology (WCIT), which was hosted by George Mason University in June 1998. This international event is analogous to the Olympics, as thousands of information technology experts visited our campus to exchange state-of-the-art advancements in this particular field of technology. Everybody who is anybody in information technology, plus a host of international dignitaries, were on the GMU campus for three to five days in June 1998. This was an event of enormous importance to GMU for a variety of reasons; not the least of which is the fact that GMU is located in one of the most robust information technology regions in the world. The university has held itself out as a leader in technology, and its president, Alan Merten, is a nationally recognized figure in information technology. The institution also offered the first doctorate in information technology in the country. This was more than just another event at GMU, so successful event management had to become our top priority support service unit for improvement analysis.

Through our own environmental scanning, we determined investing our time and effort in enhancing a B+ grade in events management to an A grade in preparation for the WCIT event was more important than working on improving a C+ grade in another support service area. This re-prioritization of our continuous improvement process review was a conscious action based directly upon the institutional priorities of the greater university. Consequently will follow this decision, but that is what this fourth step is all about. There were several institution-wide forums to inform the university of this support service initiative. There had to be an understanding that since there are only limited resources to allocate to intense unit process reengineering, those resources were being directed in a manner consistent with the immediate goals and objectives of the university.

Resist the temptation to skip over this step. Just as we warned you that you will be tempted to bypass the steps where you identify the universe of support services and the reason for providing the service in the first place, you will be tempted here to bypass the mapping/scanning for best practices and jump into the selection of alternative delivery systems. (See Figure 11.) It is a

Figure 11
SELECTING ALTERNATIVE DELIVERY SYSTEMS

Step	Tempted to Skip	Advice
1. Identify	High X	Just Do It
2. Question	High X	Just Do It
3. Evaluate		Cool Your Jets
4. Scan/Map	High X	Just Do It
5. Select		Cool Your Jets

natural temptation to simply want to evaluate (Step 3) and select an alternative system (Step 5). If you fall to this temptation you may make a quick delivery system decision, but you will have done so at great peril to your institution.

In closing this chapter, we re-emphasize that environmental scanning is an essential prerequisite to your success in the selection of a route toward a best practice service. Your environmental scanning is an all-inclusive, comprehensive review of the alpha–omega universe of possible factors that could affect your journey toward a best practice support service. This will provide you with a complete and fully integrated environmental statement. Get out from behind your desk! Leave the campus! Learn as much as you can learn ... then learn a little more. After you take your best shot at a best practice the learning must continue.

9

Step 5: Analyze and Select the Route

THE FIVE-STEP UNIT REVIEW PROCESS

Step	Function/Activity
1	Identify Universe
2	Determine Rationale
3	Evaluate Performance
4	Map/Scan Environment
5	**Select the Route**

The fifth and final step in selecting a best practice system of delivery is making the actual decision to restructure, discontinue the service, outsource, or continue with current operations. This step requires your most critical thinking. Anything less will most assuredly doom the effort. For every institution the weights and measures are a little different, but the best practice decision you are about to make is more of a business decision with substantial personnel implications than it is a personnel decision with substantial business implications. This is why the five-step unit review process includes such a heavy dose of business process reengineering (BPR) type analyses.

At every step of the way, you must be cognizant of the potential personnel ramifications, but the desire to establish best practice services must be your primary driver. By the fifth step of the process, you will have a much better understanding of your staff than you had before undertaking this unit review. This knowledge should accurately reflect your staff's ability and willingness to be part of your change team of the future. This information will be invaluable to you as you weigh your service delivery options. Your personnel are often your greatest asset in this business decision analysis.

Objective Analysis

You should also have a much better read on the future prospects of each support service. You should know where each service industry is going, and who are the leaders in each support service industry. Step 4 may not have answered all of your questions, but you should be in a better position to begin an information-driven analysis to assist answering critical questions. For instance, does it really make sense for the university to expend time and effort providing a service that is not the core mission of the institution? Is someone else in private industry providing the same service to other totally satisfied colleges or universities?

Having traversed through the first four steps of the process, you now have a much better perspective of the niche that this support service holds in the greater college and university picture. You and your staff have a heightened awareness of where the institution is going, and a much better understanding of the potential, even-tangential consequences of any changes within this service unit. What is crucial at this juncture is your just-concluded, comprehensive environmental scanning findings. You have identified the target; the question is how best to reach it.

With the fifth step comes the risk of being overtaken by emotionalism and personalization. Since some of the alternative systems of service delivery to be analyzed could possibly end the employment of existing staff in their current positions, you must continue the process in a business-like fashion. At this point in the process things become very personal, so your ability to be sensitive and caring is crucial. The selection of a best practices route will have personnel consequences. Collectively we should celebrate the opportunity to recast university support services. Keep in mind that the greater your distance from the friendly confines of home, the more likely you are to stall out or run out of gas. You must manage the process, especially down the home stretch. It is your responsibility to see that the process continues through this final step, and the key to your success is your ability and commitment to effectively communicate with the staff on a regular and routine basis as you proceed through these final steps.

Lesson 96

You cannot linger at this stage of deciding upon the future method of service delivery. There is a sense of urgency, and the staff must see it in every action you take.

Assuming that your college or university is still considering alternatives and remains uncertain about which delivery system represents a best practice, a thorough analysis must be completed during the fifth stage before the actual selection. Fortunately, much of your internal operations environmental scanning has already been completed during Step 4. Here is the kind of environmental scanning that you must analyze in this final step:

Personnel:

- You know your people, and you know their capabilities. Are they the people that can take you where you need to go with this support service?

- Are you dealing with labor contracts, unions, severance pay, several near-term retirements, etc.?

- Does a decision to outsource create new, advanced employment opportunities for displaced university staff?

- Are there alternative employment opportunities within the institution, or in the immediate surrounding area, for those that would be displaced with a change in delivery?

- Is regional or local unemployment a concern with a decision to outsource?

- Can you guarantee redeployment opportunities within the organization to displaced staff, if they agree to job adaptability and professional training?

Economic Development:

- What would be the economic impact both within the college or university and outside the immediate region, if you changed delivery systems?

- Is regional unemployment a major factor in the area?

Institutional Philosophy:

- What is the governing board's position on outsourcing?
- What is the board's position on the delegation of authority to corporate partners?
- What is the culture within the institution?
- Are other outsourced activities operating effectively within the college or university?
- Has the college or university's experience with integrating contractors with staff to improve support services been positive or negative?

Service Availability:

- What does the region offer in terms of alternatives?
- Does the area have successful private firms providing the desired services?
- Are these firms currently providing the service to other colleges or universities?
- Have these outside contractors expressed interest in providing the service to the college or university?

Timing and Vulnerability:

- Are the market conditions conducive to providing competitive responses to the request?
- Have recent occurrences in the industry made it a bull or bear market?
- Is now a good time to buy?
- Can the institution cope with a less than smooth transition if you change delivery systems?
- Have you objectively assessed the consequences of a poor decision?
- Do you have the institutional strength to recover quickly?

As mentioned earlier, much of this environmental scanning should have been accomplished during the fourth step. If necessary, use the fifth step to fill in any holes in the scanning and mapping, and then look to select your route.

Constantly remind your staff why you are looking at alternative ways to provide the service. The reason—a quest for best practice—should be obvious, but sometimes we forget to remind staff of the rationale for the analysis. The ultimate objective of the search is always similar but the more generally recognized (on-campus) reasons for looking for service improvement are not always the same. The differences in the institutional rationale for embarking on a particular service review are often quite significant. For instance, you may be convinced that one service is simply not performing in a financially acceptable manner, and you are looking to determine if any other alternate delivery systems are providing the service in a more financially acceptable manner. Another service being provided on campus may not be able to attract sufficient numbers of professional staff to provide the service. You must share your vision continuously to effectively proceed through this fifth element step.

Clarity of purpose will result in solutions from the most unexpected sources. For instance, do not be surprised to see interest from firms that you never thought had such a support service division, or were even making a move toward entering your area of service need. You may also receive expressions of interest from creative and innovative groups from within your own organization. Keep a watchful eye on changes in service regulations— either federal, state, or local. These potential bureaucratic requirements should receive your consideration when looking at delivery system alternatives. At GMU, when we look at the viability of other corporate entities to provide a given service, we expect and encourage creative partnerships from within the university family. We have often found that this functional unit review process provides greater clarity and focus to our own front line managers, which results in internal restructuring proposals from university staff to address the newly understood objectives of the institution.

Timing, Timing, Timing

A critical feature of the selection step is an assessment of the timing. As experienced business officers, you know that the best decisions can turn sour if made at the wrong time, and the riskiest decisions can look genius if made at the right time. Following this step-by-step approach provides most of the information you need to determine if the timing is good or bad for a decision to change your system of delivery.

First, you must assess your situation on your campus. If you are contemplating a major change in how you provide a given service, you must anticipate a less-than-smooth transition. Can the college or university absorb a bump in the road at this time? Consider the internal workload. Where you have the flexibility, try to avoid having several major services come up for review at the same time. The best practice review process can be very burdensome and, if not managed, you can accumulate such a volume of service review responsibilities that you just have more than can be humanly accomplished at any one given time.

------------------------------   **Lesson 97**   ------------------------------

Regardless of your current system of delivery (self-operation or outsourced), you should develop a multi-year master service review schedule. This master schedule will allow you to schedule these service review processes throughout each year.

For example, when we hosted the World Congress on Information Technology, we did not plan for summer of 1998 provider changes in any support service activities that could even remotely jeopardize the successful management of this event. Our internal assessment was more comprehensive than simply determining if there was a show stopper kind of event that should defer us from engaging in any other major restructuring initiatives. You must, however, determine your institution's capacity to assume increased risk and exposure.

At GMU we carefully and routinely assess our institutional vulnerability capacity. For instance, are there other major restructuring activities going on within the university that depend on the stability of certain support services to effectively navigate their transition? Reservations about implementing a service change do not stem from the fact that other restructuring is on-going, since restructuring is always happening throughout the campus. However, you should have reservations if your level of restructuring activity could jeopardize the delivery of essential services.

------------------------------ **Lesson 98** ------------------------------

The need to pause and possibly delay a major restructuring initiative may simply be an acknowledgment that the institution cannot absorb any additional risk or vulnerability in its support services at this partic-ular time. Don't exceed your capacity. Rome was not built in a day!

On the issue of timing, you must assess the competitive market place. Determine if your operation is attractive to those in the market place, and decide if there is sufficient competition to ensure an opportunity to compare alternative options. For example, the university bookstore market has changed dramatically over the past 10 years. Beginning in the late 1970s and continuing through the early 1990s, GMU could depend on a substantial num-ber (four to eight) of university bookstore contract proposals. The industry has changed however and, depending on your location, you can no longer expect more than three offers, with two firms really controlling the industry. This is neither an advantage nor a disadvantage for universities, but simply a change and you must be fully aware of its consequences as it may impact your choice of a service delivery system.

We have developed a market-sensitive general rule of thumb. If we are not fully satisfied with the level of competition in the market, we will not extend a contract beyond three years. In this type of limited competition envi-ronment, we are most likely to opt for a two or three year contract with two or three one-year options. Even in the best of competitive situations, we tend to shy away from contracts that commit the parties beyond five years. We have never negotiated a contract for more than 10 years, and our only 10-year con-tract involved a very unique set of circumstances that have not been replicated since the early 1980s.

The following examples, drawn from GMU's experiences in different support service areas, illustrate how timing influences every search for best practice.

Timing! (Food Services)

In 1985, we were in the midst of changing food service contractors. The firm we had engaged for the past 10 years had performed in a commendable fashion, but it was clear that the students were tired of the food service pro-vided by the current contractor. This is certainly not a surprising attitude to find on any college campus. Where the students helped us immeasurably was in the way they focused their concern on the quality of the food. That registered with the selection team, and we became more active in seeking the interest of certain high food quality corporate partners. For example, in our own backyard we have the corporate headquarters of a major food service contractor, and they had previously expressed their interest in the GMU contract. Although they had been unsuccessful in procuring our business in the past, we made sure they knew we were interested in seeing a proposal from them.

It was both the name recognition and the firm's generally recognized reputation in the region as a quality food provider that became pivotal factors in our selection decision. At this particular time in our history, we were not going to select a firm that didn't have quality name recognition. We were looking for a firm with an established reputation for high quality. In other support services at other times, we were looking for totally different characteristics in our prospective partner. On occasion we have actually searched for selected firms with marginal experience in the field of higher education, but with a creative and innovative vision of the future. You must know what qualities you need from a corporate partner at a particular time.

As a consequence of the food service corporation's name recognition, we continue to give greater latitude to the use of their corporate name on campus than we do most other corporate partners. Our food service is known as George Mason University Dining Services, but most students also know the name of the corporation that provides the food service. We continue to believe this says something positive about the university's commitment to provide the students a high quality food service.

Timing! (Dining and Recreation)

The important thing about timing is that time never stands still! GMU has a small shopping mall right across the street from the campus. The mall offers a mid-priced restaurant, a discount priced, second-run movie theater, and a relaxed atmosphere within easy walking distance of the campus. In recent years both the restaurant and the movie theater aggressively catered to the needs of GMU students. Ten years ago, however, the mall was under different management, and its restaurant and movie theater paid no attention to the needs of GMU students, faculty, and staff. At the time, GMU was seriously considering creating its own on-campus restaurant and movie theater to fill the void.

Over the years, however, the new owners of these shops forged a solid relationship with GMU. As much as one could possibly expect, the mall restaurant and movie theater are seen as an extension of the university. Faculty and staff dine frequently at the restaurant, where most of the sandwiches carry the name of a GMU personality. The theater admits GMU students, faculty, and staff at a reduced fee when they show their university identification. Several businesses in this mall now accept Mason Money, which is another strong indication of their desire to cater to the needs of our students. In this case, the university avoided both a major cost and duplication of service by deferring to the expertise of these shopping mall entrepreneurs, and as a natural by-product, a mutually beneficial partnership has been established between the university and these two business enterprises.

------------------------------ **Lesson 99** ------------------------

The element of timing is inseparable and inescapably embodied within both environmental scanning and decision making.

Timing! (Student Housing)

In 1989, our student housing RFP contained three separate sub-service module—maintenance/housekeeping, operational management, and residential life—and offerors could bid on any of the three. We expected our marketing efforts to bring in some good competition, but most of the proposals came from local property rental type organizations. Only one company bid on the entire package, and it later withdrew its bid. We found none of the offers very attractive, so we decided to manage both the operation and residential life components ourselves, and we outsourced only maintenance and housekeeping. Other ancillary services including grounds and security services related to student housing were outsourced a few years later.

Then in 1995, management of all student-housing functions was contracted to a firm with hospitality and hotel experience that had just been formed as a result of the merger of two companies. The market is slowly improving in terms of service providers. By the time we released the 1998 housing RFP, we had the opportunity to select from several highly competitive offers.

Lesson 100

Just because you are ready to go to market doesn't mean the market is ready for you.

Timing! (Banking)

As a part of your review of the issue of timing, consider not only what has been happening in the industry, but also what appears to be about to happen in the industry. This is especially important today, when it seems like a new corporate merger occurs every month. You may not be able to gather data on every potential merger, but if the current management of the service provider is a determinative factor to you in your selection, you would be well advised to discuss any such concerns before you award the contract.

For example, we knew of the merger trend occurring in the banking industry, but we dropped the ball during our on-campus banking selection process. Although we don't know whether any merger information would have been divulged at the time, we should have incorporated language in the contract to specifically address the possibility of a merger within the first months of a new contract. At a minimum, we should have engaged the offerors in a serious conversation about any potential merger. We did neither! A few short months after selecting a local bank, it merged with an out-of-state bank and took the out-of-state bank's name. We do not anticipate any long-term problem and we will work through their transition, but we should have known better. We have already experienced some unexpected bumps in the road that may have been totally avoidable had we done a better job of scanning the environment of the banking industry.

Corporate Compatibility

As you consider alternative delivery systems for support services, it is important to understand not only what is going on in the industry, but also the key corporate characteristics of the firms in a particular support service industry. You will not (and would not want to) find a corporate replica of your institutional profile and culture, but can you find a compatible corporate partner? You must!

When considering outsourcing as an option, you need to explore the possibility of mission melding with any other external service providing entity. For example, when the then dean of students, Donald Mash, and director of business services, Larry Czarda, led a university team in reviewing the possibility of outsourcing the Patriot Center, we needed to resist the temptation of being attracted by the firms that could guarantee the greatest net profits. We had no interest in cashing in on every early revenue opportunity that could have been generated by any prospective corporate partner. In our initial years, it was paramount that we establish the Patriot Center as a suburban venue for university and family entertainment. We were not driven solely to make a lot of money by blindly booking as many events as possible.

The priorities for use of the facility were detailed in the original RFP. We wanted a balanced array of entertainment events while leaving room for our basketball program and other institutional events such as graduation ceremonies. The highest priority was regularly scheduled university events followed by proprietary events scheduled by the contractor, and approved by the university events management. As the owner, we knew we were going to be selective in what we hosted and we needed to retain complete event approval.

---------------------- **Lesson 101** ----------------------

Where significant differences in mission exist between organizational partners, clarity from both partners is essential in all communications regarding shared responsibilities.

Service Consequences—Broadly Defined

Many support service contracts are broader than you think and overlap to a great degree with other services provided in-house or outsourced. The interrelationship of one service to others is often not understood by contractors and not adequately explained by the institution. If you do not fully explain these interrelationships in your RFP, you have set yourself up for a classic case of the left hand not knowing what the right hand is doing. In our national research, we have often been struck by how inadequate the language has been in many of the RFPs relative to identifying related services. Compounding the problem has been the fact that many universities do not distribute RFPs to affected university parties.

Lesson 102

When eliciting interest in your support service requirements, it is incumbent upon the university to not only identify all related inter-dependent support service players but to share this inter-departmental information with the actual university players on your campus.

Your institutional philosophies should be included in the RFP. When an institution looks to outsource, its senior administration must understand that the mission and objectives of the contractor are not always consistent with those of the institution. While priorities of the contractor and institution may coincide, the contractor is more likely to place a greater emphasis on short-term objectives at the expense of long-term goals. You must enter partnerships with the realization and understanding that the goals and objectives of firms are not and never will be totally consistent with those of a college or university. This should be a healthy point of friction, but if you fail to constantly remind yourself of this nuance within the partnership, you begin to lose focus, control, and direction within your outsourced services.

Each institution must decide on the proper balance between institutional and corporate philosophies on such diverse criteria as organizational mission, management control, operational performance, cost of services to the customers, organizational culture, quality of service, customer relations, investment in infrastructure, technology strategies, and financial return to the institution.

Lesson 103

The decision process involves the identification and assessment of the trade-offs between alternatives. In the end, the decision should be based on which strengths of the prospective partner most closely match the needs and priorities of your organization.

For instance, we have found that food service firms are excellent at projecting costs, but not as skilled at projecting revenue from new sources, for which they tend to be overly conservative. They are much more apt to say that new sales are simply substitution sales and they tend to be reluctant to project that there is a greater universe of sales beyond current sales. Again, if understood, this shortcoming can be a healthy point of friction.

Lesson 104

In creative service partnerships, it is not unhealthy for your enthusiasm for change to be met by your corporate partner's conservative mindset of operational cost consciousness. When these two perspectives collide, the result should be a well-reasoned decision.

10

The High-Five Management Approach

As confident as we are that our five-step unit review process will give you your best shot at hitting that elusive target of service excellence, it is not a sure thing. The key to your success rests not in religiously following the step-by-step approach but in your capacity to embrace a culture of change at your institution. If you envision your quest for best practices as building an arrow, then you can see that the five-step unit review process is only the arrowhead. The arrowhead is strong because it is made from the accurate, objective, fully integrated information you gathered during the five-step process. If we can get this arrowhead to hit the target on its own, it will undoubtedly penetrate and stick.

But to improve its odds of hitting the target, the arrow needs stability in flight. The high-five approach to best practices adds the shaft and the feathers to the arrowhead created in the five-step unit review process. The high-five management approach is made up of five I's:

- Integrity
- Insight
- Inspiration
- Intimacy
- Integrity

Lessons of the past have taught us that during our pioneering journey for excellence we will be constantly challenged, criticized, and ostracized as we attempt to pursue avenues for institutional improvement that have never been previously undertaken. This cynicism will most likely increase substantially as we endure through our mistakes, errors of judgment, and unpopular decisions. We have found that the best way to not only survive but to excel during both good times and bad times, is to incorporate an institutional approach (or organizational culture) that is built on these five qualities, each of which is described in greater detail below.

Integrity

The order of the high-five elements is important! Integrity, our first element, is the shaft of the arrow. It is the single, most important, non-negotiable characteristic of this approach to change management. If you already have it (which in a business setting is determined by the perception of others), use it as your ally as you engage in your ongoing search for best practice. If you do not have it, you have to attain it! For those of you that have personally lost the perception of integrity with the staff, or have inherited a situation where the staff simply doesn't believe that management has any integrity—there is still hope! Your hope rests in your capacity to objectively engage in a search for excellence in an open, honest manner. Can you loosen your tight-fisted grip on the reigns of support service control? Can you give others a voice in the future of the support services of the institution? If the answer is yes, regained integrity is within your reach.

The high-five management approach adopts integrity as its foundation, because managing and searching for best practices during periods of change, uncertainty, and chaos will require an unwavering core characteristic immune from the pressures of the politically correct and the don't rock the boat contingencies that exist at most institutions. At George Mason University we have defined institutional integrity as a commitment to do the right thing. Consider all the input and weigh all the information available! Then make the decision that is in the best interests of the university. Personal, departmental, and divisional agendas must be set aside in favor of the institution.

We believe that how we manage information is often illustrative of our level of corporate integrity. Is it a resource that we covet or a resource we share? At GMU we have changed a common, and highly restrictive, need to know attitude about sharing information to a new "if you care, glad to share" perspective on information. We feel integrity is synonymous with full disclosure. It is probably not possible to nurture an integrity-first community where we are unwilling to share throughout the organization the more important corporate information. Integrity is the confidence to let loose of the reigns of control. There is no question that information is power. The question is: Are we willing and able to share the power? We think many college and university administrators find this information-sharing concept to be foreign and quite unappealing. The high-five approach suggests that it is time to break out of these old ways of thinking and bring in the new.

Your staff is the integrity that gives the arrow its stability, while the arrowhead provides the information that gives the arrow its strength. At this point we have built the body of the arrow. Now we must build its spirit. What type of feathers will enable it to retain accuracy during flight and keep the arrow true to its course over the greatest of distance and during the worst of weather conditions? The feathers of the arrow are the remaining four I's. Without an organizational commitment to these four management qualities, your capacity to achieve service excellence will be substantially diminished.

Insight

This task of leadership in the 21st century is no easy assignment. Let's take a quick look at the picture again. We seem to have some idea of where we are going, but we are not sure if we will be satisfied once we get there. No one has been there before, so we have no roadmap or footprints to follow. The only thing we know for certain is that we cannot afford to stay in the place we are in right now. On top of these elements of uncertainty, every day it seems we find ourselves competing with a set of brand new players. You cannot recognize any of the players or even some of the teams without a game day program.

In that type of environment, you must somehow provide the focus and the insight to effectively manage your college or university through change toward best practices. It will be easy to be overwhelmed, and the natural tendency will be to search for protective cover. It will be easy for you to be distracted, and it will be even easier for the other members of the organization to be distracted. We live in a complex world, and we are individually and collectively often distracted in our professional lives by either other workplace demands or other personal priorities. These distractions are often stress additives which certainly complicate the efforts of the change-agent leadership of the organization.

Lesson 105

As the leader, you must be sensitive to the push-pull emotional realities associated with restructuring, reengineering, and reorganization, and yet skillful enough to keep the organization on course. This is the management skill of coaching or steering, and is most effective when organizational insight is the conceptual driver.

To meet this challenge of effective management today, we must be fearless in navigating through the necessary detours of this journey for best practices. It is crucial during these detours that we have the self-discipline to recognize and differentiate between mindless drifting and strategic maneuvering. We cannot lose sight of our objective. As mentioned in chapter 1, we must be able to distinguish windows of opportunities from hallways of distraction.

Insight, like integrity, requires not only information-sharing, but full disclosure. We must answer the questions of where are we going and why are we going there. Giving the answer once is not sufficient; we must provide the answers to these questions on a regular and routine manner. You will never over-reassure the staff on organizational purpose and direction. When you are uncertain about the next move, there is no shame in sharing the uncertainty. You haven't lost sight of the target, you could simply use some help or need some time before deciding upon the next course of action. We are all in this together. No one expects you to be the all-knowing leader of the world. They already know that there is no such person anywhere in the organization.

So why do so many business officers continue to put on this "I am in control . . . full speed ahead" facade? That is not what the troops are looking for in today's leader. They are expecting, often demanding, that management provide open and honest communication on where you are going; what you are trying to accomplish; why you are taking this course of action; and to the extent possible, how do you intend to accomplish the objective. Share the vision!

Lesson 106

Keep the target in sight and the organization in sync. Everyone can contribute, and some can even help steer, if the organization continues to provide the insight.

Inspiration

Sounds corny! There certainly is no prescription for this organizational quality or corporate characteristic in the management of your organization. Good managers know that what inspires employee A may not have a similar affect on employee B, and may actually turn off or offend employee C. But this complicating factor is not a reason to discard the need to nurture this characteristic in your organizational culture. The complexity of the skill set simply warns you that there is no easy cookie-cutter answer to keeping the staff committed to the mission of the organization.

We all know of great speakers who can emotionally move large audiences, and we have all listened to outstanding orators who have inspired us to strive for greater achievements. Most people, however, have not been blessed with such a set of inspirational skills. Fortunately, this is not the kind of inspiration needed to move organizations to greater achievements. If we can learn when a pat on the back is in order, and when (metaphorically speaking) a swift kick in the butt is necessary, then we have grasped the kind of inspiration needed in our organizations. You will learn when you need to pick someone up who has fallen, and when you must allow the person to rise without your assistance. These are never easy calls to make.

Inspiration is knowing when to light a candle and when to start a bonfire. Inspiration is developing a deft touch. Inspiration is the essence of leadership! Insight may help the organization set its sights on a common goal, but inspiration is essential to achieving individual and organizational action. Once we have shared the vision and given the insight, we must inspire team members to take the journey and nurture them along the way.

Intimacy

The fourth element in the high-five approach to management is intimacy. We initially debated this management characteristic, because it sounded a little too touchy-feely. It has, however, survived as one of the key elements of our management culture, because it is so pervasive in the way we search for support service best practices. In the first chapters of this book, we reinforced the importance of getting to know what you were doing in your support services. We emphasized understanding the interrelationships between our support services, and we always enlisted our best and brightest staff to conduct our functional unit reviews.

In Step 3 of the five-step unit review process, we suggested that you rigorously assess why you were providing the service. This up-close and personal style continued through Step 4, where we scanned the universe for possible best practices. In fact, the entire review process is all about intimacy! First it is product/service intimacy, then it shifts to personnel intimacy, and throughout the process it embraces customer intimacy. There is no alternative! This search for service excellence is never an arms-length approach toward service improvement. Intimacy ensures understanding, and understanding leads to decisions resulting in improvement.

Intensity

The final element—the last of the five I's in the high-five approach—is intensity. This element actually was one of the first elements that we discovered when we took a close look at what we perceived to be the strengths of our organizational culture. At one time or another, we have all wanted to begin cloning our best and most passionate staff members. Although we seem to have little difficulty in identifying our outstanding performers, we sure have a tough time increasing the number of them. We think we have learned something about making this passion a little more contagious in your organization.

First of all, without your highly visible, personal passion for your own organizational search for excellence, there is no chance for the organization as a whole to grasp the excitement and passion associated with the journey. However, as important as it appears that intensity is in the formula for organizational improvement, it is not the target. This intense desire to succeed that we see in our best staff is simply an easily visible byproduct of a whole set of other more important workplace variables. We must understand that the passion and the intensity that can consume an entire organization and move it toward service excellence is for the most part motivated by something or someone else.

We believe that intensity is a by-product of an organizational culture that is:

- founded upon an unwavering principle of integrity;
- committed to regular communications on organizational focus and insight;
- embedded in a philosophy of timely and meaningful inspiration;

- unashamed and driven by the need to achieve increasingly greater service intimacy; and

- wed to the belief that since time is always of the essence, the search for best practices will be undertaken with great vigor.

Our five-step approach for best practices is a fully integrated, information-driven process that will consistently provide you with your best shot at the best practice target. However, although our best practice process demands input diversity, environmental scanning, critical thinking, and rigorous self-evaluation, it does not guarantee an organizational change of culture. That is why we advocate blending the high-five management approach with this recommended unit review, best practices search process.

Our premise is that the only organizational journey worth taking is one that moves the organization. Since we know that the search for best practices is by definition an endless journey, we must achieve an organizational culture where tomorrow's leaders are just as driven to embrace change and search for best practices as today's leaders. We know that tomorrow's searchers will be different than today's. So our goal must be organizational in nature—not merely individualistic. There is no question that the target is to change the culture of the organization. Our quest, therefore, is to permeate the high-five culture throughout the organization, thereby ensuring that organizationally we will never be totally satisfied with today's accomplishments. The search for best practices must always continue.

Part III:

Lessons from the Journey

Now, when you have formed a team of partnership between your contract administrators and the institution's management, you need to help them reach optimal performance and apply the lessons learned. The key to successful management teams and partnerships is knowledge of your personnel.

11

Applying Lessons Learned

As emphasized throughout this book, blending partnerships between private industry firms and colleges and universities involves many challenges. The key components of a successful partnership are:

- communication on a routine and regular basis;
- joint ownership and responsibility for both the process and the product;
- an understanding of and respect for the fact that the organizational objectives of the partners are not the same.

Having this partner by your side must be considered an asset and not a liability, as you now attempt to accomplish the objectives of your institutional support services. Think of the classic police scenario where two officers arrive at the scene of the crime, and need to find out whether the criminals are still in the building. With weapons drawn, one crouches down and takes a few steps forward to make sure that everything is clear on the right. The other officer does the same thing in a criss-cross fashion and checks to make sure everything is clear on the left. This buddy system continues until the officers either find the criminals or determine that they have left the premises. Both officers understand the benefits of the partnership, and have complete confidence in their partner's ability. Officer A doesn't do what he or she knows officer B is supposed to be doing. Similarly, without this element of trust and understanding in your outsourcing arrangement, you will not reap the benefits of a partnership alliance.

The biggest challenge most colleges and universities face will be their institutional capacity to share rather than control decision-making responsibility without losing sight of their ultimate accountability. Such a balancing act is not a common practice within higher education, and it certainly will not be very comfortable for many institutions.

You outsource to gain the advantage brought by someone else—give them some space! In this chapter we will discuss the never-ending need to adjust our sights to improve our chances of hitting the target. We will also talk about who should take the shot in certain situations. We will show you that under certain circumstances, some personnel in this partnership should never have any arrows in their quiver. The performance of any support service will have its moments of truth, where the service has to be the best it can be. For the most part these moments do not come unexpectedly. We see them in the distance, which certainly is fortunate, but when the time arrives we still must deliver with an optimal service performance. Our best shot at meeting these challenges comes in knowing the strengths and weaknesses within the partnership.

Whenever a college or university selects a private corporation or firm with whom to partner, it must first completely and objectively assess its own strengths and weaknesses as illustrated through the five-step unit review process. For instance, when GMU partnered with a corporate firm to operate and manage student housing, we did not look for a firm with a track record of strength in student discipline, nor did we look for a firm with financial management prowess. The university had existing staff with strength in these two areas, but it had been unable to incorporate housing into the fabric of student life on campus or develop a maintenance response system that treated student housing occupants as guests of the university. These were our weaknesses, so we looked for a firm with strengths in these areas. Colleges and universities must make known their strengths as well as their weaknesses when they communicate with prospective partners.

Strengths and weaknesses change over the life of a partnership, and they also change based upon the particular circumstances. The college or university must be aware of these peculiarities within each of its partnerships. Partnerships face the same struggles as we find daily when staff members cannot work together to arrive at a mutually satisfactory solution. The solution exists in such cases, but if the parties involved do not have the skills (or wills) to work together, they will never find it. Living in a constantly changing environment makes these partnerships and staff interrelationships even more difficult.

"You cannot step twice into the same river, other and still other waters flow upon them."

—Heraclitus

Acknowledging that certain offices, or individuals within those offices, cannot see the world in the same way can often help you to develop a strategy for maximizing a relationship that otherwise could become strained and unproductive. You must take a proactive role in nurturing this relationship. It is naive to think that individuals from different organizations with substantially different missions will just naturally mesh into compatible partnerships!

Lesson 107

Once the partnership is consummated you must understand that this teaming together for the greater good will never just happen naturally. Like any other marriage, both organizations will have to work diligently on the relationship to ensure that the two organizations retain focus on a shared vision.

You and each of your contract administrators must understand that not all individuals within each of these entities can effectively team to achieve the greater benefit for the college and university. This does not mean that the individuals involved are any less valuable to the organization. It simply means that some offices, and some individuals are like oil and water. To help them reach optimal performance, you may have to intervene with a facilitator, an arbiter—or in the worse case, work around the problem.

The key to successful management teams and partnerships is knowledge of your personnel. You cannot know too much about your team's strengths and weaknesses, nor can you know too much about the strengths and weaknesses of your corporate partner. At GMU, we learn early in each of our partnerships about those individuals and those situations that should either be avoided, or need to be closely monitored. Paying attention to those businesses that have been outsourced to a corporate partner carries no less responsibility.

For example, if you know your food service manager is not a strong financial person, you do not want her to be the one who provides you the financial pro-forma on your new idea to begin a satellite point of food service delivery. If your bookstore manager is not a big-picture person, you probably do not want him to be the point person on arranging a book signing opportunity for an author who happens to be the best friend of the president's wife. If you know the strengths and weaknesses of the personnel of your partner, you can support, and sometimes even encourage, the efforts of your corporate partner to provide the professional development opportunities to address any weaknesses.

---------------------------------- **Lesson 108** ----------------------

Team chemistry is crucial to every partnership success, and a prerequisite to building team chemistry is player compatibility. Know your personnel and attain/maintain a better understanding of your partner's personnel.

This knowledge and understanding, however, is only the first step in building team chemistry. The next step is learning to manage, direct, and orchestrate the efforts of our partnerships. We like to compare this aspect of building team chemistry to the selection process for professional golf's Ryder Cup competition. The first task in Ryder Cup selection process is a tough one: identifying the 18 greatest golfers in the United States. But the second task— putting these great golfers in two-person teams to compete against the best European golfers—is by far the more difficult challenge. A portion of this event includes a competition where one member of each two-person team takes the first shot, his partner takes the second shot, and the rotation continues throughout the match. For eighteen holes, one team player takes his shot from the location left by his partner's shot. Imagine the ebb and flow of emotions throughout the day, as each of your shots is totally determined by the previous shot of your partner. Building a strong national team of professional golfers is much more about determining the compatibility of each golfer's mental and emotional approach to the game than it is about evaluating each player's golf shot expertise.

The Ryder Cup selection process remind us that even when we have a full and complete understanding of the members of the team, we cannot assume that we have the players in the positions necessary to ensure success. We need to determine whom we can rely upon to get the process back on track after the wheels fall off, which like the stray golf shot, is bound to happen as we deal with uncertainty, change, and a little chaos.

The C's of Success

We have shared with our staff that it is not by coincidence that the word success is anchored by a double letter "c" in the middle of the word. We are

Figure 12 **SUCCESS**	
• Challenging	• Compatibility
• Commitment	• Complimentary
• Concentration	• Coordinated
• Constructive	• Communicated
• Change-oriented	• Continuous

equally convinced that the letter "c" is the lead letter in at least 10 of the most important characteristics necessary to build successful partnerships (see figure 12).

The order of the "c" words is consistent with the process that we envision when we embark on a partnership initiative. There must be focus and a willingness to attack the problem to reach a constructive solution. Team members must also possess a willingness to be pioneers, out-of-the-box solution finders, and fearless about change. The partnership must operate in a compatible, complimentary fashion, and all of its actions must be both coordinated and communicated. Last of all, it must be understood we are in this for the long run, so continuity is non-negotiable. We have come to realize, however, that the achievement of these "c" objectives hinges upon service intimacy and fresh eyes.

Lesson 109

Contentment may start with the letter "c," but this word is not part of our formula for partnership success. There is no time to rest on yesterday's laurels. We are always raising the bar or having it raised by someone else.

Focus on Objectivity

When we wanted to restructure our publications and media relations, we looked to our vice president for university relations, Helen Ackerman, to lead the unit review. She knew the operation, and she knew it was time for a new approach. Among her greatest assets were her willingness to close down the distance between fact and fiction and eliminate the generalities associated with rumors and anecdotal stories. She recognized as her weakness, a natural tendency to see issues from the personnel perspective rather than the business perspective, and an almost blind loyalty to her staff. To compensate for this weakness, she surrounded herself with best practice search team members who constantly brought creative and innovative business possibilities forward for discussion. She put together a team with balance. As a university relations executive, she soon brought her own fresh eyes into the process. She was initially somewhat stymied by her overwhelming concern for the welfare of her existing staff, but she came to see the restructuring options not as threats to her employees, but as opportunities for attaining excellence in her support services.

What allowed her to turn the corner? She realized that this unit review was not being driven by personnel-related concerns, but by a desire to pursue whatever strategies necessary to make university relations operation as good as it could be. The excitement that consumes a team when it fully realizes its own potential is a sight for sore eyes. As a result of this team's transformation, the function of university relations has been totally reconstructed. Parts of the operation have been contracted to a corporate partner, while other parts are provided by university staff with totally revamped job descriptions. Some employees previously employed within university relations have assumed challenging new positions within other areas of the university, while others have left the university and are gainfully employed outside the university. Service intimacy and fresh eyes!

> *"The real voyage of discovery consists not in seeking new lands,*
> *but in seeing with new eyes."*
>
> —Marcel Proust

Objectivity was the advantage our vice president for university relations had in directing this assignment. Whether before selecting a corporate partner or during the management of the partnership, the responsible university administrator must be seen as an objective party in all matters concerning operational effectiveness. In the university relations example, we saw how a university administrator's objectivity allowed her to effectively lead her team through the functional review exercise and towards a best practice solution. An experienced, attentive contract administrator can be equally effective in strengthening a partnership if astute enough to see the weak linkages in the relationship. The contract administrator can help each party better understand what the other party is trying to accomplish, but this can only be achieved if the contract administrator is perceived as neither an advocate nor a detractor of the outsourced firm or business entity.

Accomplishing this neutrality and objectivity is no easy task for the contract administrator, because the college and university community tends to view this person as an advocate for the corporate partner and a zealot for outsourcing and privatization. The effective contract administrator must develop a decision-making track record that illustrates fair and equitable deliberations and decisions. The track record must include actions that support the position of the college and university staff, as well as actions that favor the interests of the corporate partner service provider.

The Value-Added Partnership

The partnership is all about the principle of value added. If neither party is adding value, there is no rationale for the service outsourcing agreement. Most institutions tend to be much more rigorous in their evaluation of the value being added by the corporate partner than they are of themselves. If the evaluation ends there, we most likely will miss an equally attractive opportunity. How can we enhance our contribution? We must ask ourselves, "What value are we bringing to the partnership?" More importantly, we must ask our partner, "What value do you think we bring to the relationship?" A novel approach—and one you likely have not thought of before—but the conversation that results from such a question will have unlimited potential.

All of the quantum leap advances of our partnerships can be discovered in the pioneering recesses of our innovative minds. But they can only be realized if we are open to criticism, change, and control softening. If we are really operating as partners, why are we so reluctant to ask for our partner's evaluation of our value to the partnership? These service partnerships are severely limited if one partner (typically the college or university) assumes the exclusive decision-making role in the partnership. When the partnership is consummated, both parties understand that this is a service being provided for the college and university with the assistance of a corporate partner. All of your service providers understand that they are serving the university. Your partners know they are working for you, so loosen up a little on the reigns of control! We need to shed the typical control freak paranoia personified by some of our educational institutions. We must shed our impulse to control everything if we are to reap the benefits of this venture. We need to listen to what our partner is telling us about the partnership and be ready to hear how we may be hindering the delivery of our own support service. This listening and learning is our quantum leap opportunity. Isn't a shot at excellence worth a bruised ego?

If you're interested solely in contracting with a firm to provide a service, and you are certain that existing college and university procedures, policies,

and personnel are near-perfect and will remain that way—you should negotiate a straightforward contract to achieve that service. Maybe you do not need
a corporate partner. There is nothing wrong with searching for an excellent
service contractor. Sometimes that is exactly what you need. When you need
the toilets to stop running, you are not really looking for a partner with a thou-
sand different theories on virtual plumbing in the 21st century. On the other
hand, if you are uncertain of all of the nuances between existing institution
procedures and the desired service, and are willing to consider their modification to improve the service, then you need a partner. At GMU, our partnerships have taught us the meaning of value added. We have learned that we
must constantly evaluate and re-examine the value being added by both the
university and the corporate partner. We can only make this determination if
we are willing to seek out our partner's opinion of our contribution.

------------------------------ **Lesson 110** -------------------

You can be comfortable in the presumption that the value added by
both parties will change throughout the life of a contract. You can be
equally confident that a loss in the value of the partnership is not
always due to a deterioration in the value being added by the corporate partner. Mirror, mirror on the wall!

Re-examining the value being added by each of the partners is no different than changing the oil in your automobile every 3,000 miles. Every time
you change the oil and have the automobile serviced, you realize that the car
has responded a little differently to the most recent miles traveled. However,
through this regular maintenance you have retained a closeness to the situation. The value-added reassessment of your business partnerships is really no
different. If we have been reviewing the partnership on a regular basis, there
will be no big surprises for either party. We can be certain, however, that the
value added by a particular partner last year may not be the same value being
added today. This is why we need to evaluate this relationship routinely. From
a business perspective, the management fee you pay this corporate partner is
an out-of-pocket, real cost of doing business. It is your money, so be sure you
are spending it wisely!

Lesson 111

In addition to assessing the value being added by each party, we must also determine if we still have the same need (or give the same priority) to this service today as we may have given it yesterday.

Some of the value added that our corporate partners bring are critical contributions in areas of expertise that the college or university has no interest in developing within its own staff. Other values, or skill sets, although not present on our campus when we contracted for these services, may now be buffed, polished, and ready to shine. Sometimes this gained expertise within campus personnel occurs by design, but do not be surprised to see that it sometimes almost happens by osmosis.

Lesson 112

Partners with a passion for perfection understand the need for sharing a common knowledge base. Information not shared between partners is useless data!

Lesson 113

Value is relative and relativity changes over time. You must routinely assess strengths and weaknesses of both the partnership and your organization.

When we partnered with a facilities management firm in 1985 to operate our 10,000 seat arena, we did so because we did not want to invest the time and energy in learning how to attract professional entertainment to our new venue. We assumed we could operate the facility for our intercollegiate athletic events, but we knew the facility had much greater income potential if operated by those experienced in the entertainment business. Our intimacy with this particular partnership today may be the greatest of all of our service contracts, but not because we wish to develop the skill set necessary to take over the operation. The depth of our service intimacy reflects our understanding that in the eyes of the general public, whatever transpires within the walls of this very public facility speaks volumes about the quality and reputation of the university. Therefore, as outstanding as our service provider may be, we decide what acts of entertainment will be seen in our arena. We do not take that responsibility lightly. Filling that niche in the partnership requires a substantial amount of research and service intimacy. So although we have learned the business we have done so as a partner, not as a prospective future service-provider.

Lesson 114

Even when partnering with the greatest service providers in the world, it is still essential that you maintain service intimacy.

Similarly, years after entering into both a travel partnership and a mail service partnership, we have developed a significant level of campus expertise. This expertise was a by-product of staff involvement in the functional unit review, the search for best practices process and the eventual RFP selection activities. We have no intention to change our current system of service delivery, but we have developed sufficient institutional depth to assume operational responsibility if necessary. There has clearly been some shifting between the parties of the value being added by each to the partnership.

Lesson 115

In most partnerships there is usually no good reason to wear both a belt and suspenders. But knowing you have easy access to suspenders when your belt breaks is an indication of the strength of both your organization and the partnership. Avoid unnecessary duplication, but do not get caught with your pants down.

The lessons here are simply that we must assess both value-added and internal infrastructure strength on a regular basis. You can be assured that the weights of value-added on the balance fulcrum do not remain unchanged for any period of time. Since every contract and partnership is negotiated based upon what the parties bring to the table, and the consideration (the quid-pro-quo) being exchanged determines the pricing arrangement, you must reassess your needs based upon today's changed set of circumstances. You must regularly assess your internal strengths, and those brought to the partnership by your contract service provider. Keep your eyes open! You may have a diamond in the rough—a best practice waiting to happen—or a time bomb about to explode!

The Art of Listening

Yesterday's successful performance carries no lasting satisfaction, and we can be certain that tomorrow's success will not be attained in the same manner as today's. As we noted earlier, this is not only true because we are constantly looking for improvements in the delivery of our own service, but also because we are providing services and products to a clientele with changing interests and demands. The bottom line is that customers and their likes and dislikes change. This certainly cannot be any big surprise to us, right? This is not a big problem, as long as the organization realizes that there is no way to meet the changing needs of the customer, if the service providing institution is unable to adapt in a timely manner.

What is nice about the college or university scene, unlike most other service venues, is that the student is both the customer and the product. Since we are the provider of the services, we have an awesome opportunity to shape our own future in this industry.

Lesson 116

If we listen every day to what is being said about us and take advantage of the fact that our clients/customers are some of the brightest people in the country, we will have our hand on the pulse of our business. Listening often provides us the ultimate advantage.

We work daily with those receiving our service. What a competitive advantage we have over others that may want to compete for a market share! To get the most from this advantage, however, we must ask ourselves:

- What do we have to show for having such an advantage?

- Can we persuade others that we have attained customer intimacy?

- Do we know our customers, or are we still so arrogant that we think we do not need to listen to them, because we already know what they need?

Assuming we agree that there is something to be learned by listening to our students, the test for each of us is really quite simple. We must be able to answer yes to the following questions:

- Do we listen to, and learn from, our internal and external constituencies, including our students, faculty and staff on a regular and routine basis?

- Do we continuously evaluate what else is going on in, and outside of, the higher education market place to objectively evaluate whether a best practice service delivery system has been developed elsewhere?

- Have we built an organizational structure that allows us to respond quickly to take advantage of those mission-compatible opportunities that often arise without warning?

If we are unable to answer in the affirmative, we must ask ourselves, are we at least making progress in these areas? If we are not making progress, we most likely have serious problems of adaptability within our organization. Let's assume that we are not where we want to be, but that as an organization we are improving. What is keeping us from achieving peak performance?

Fostering a Will to Change

Sometimes the will to change simply is not pervasive within a college or university, and you may actually find that change acceptance runs counter to the long-standing culture of the entity. In many such cases, the organization is deep in tradition, well respected in the fraternity of colleges and universities, and nearly revered by others in the field. However, this homage is often related to past achievements and past successes of the alumni of the institution. Change is a tough sell at a tradition-rich institution. But the question of who will provide learning in the future and how it is to be provided is up for grabs. Can any of us expect our position in the industry to remain intact based upon our 19th and 20th century reputation? With a distracted, over-committed just-in-time, learning-oriented clientele, old brand names and worn out approaches will not be the first choice for future educational needs.

The will to embrace change in even the most entrepreneurial university will not represent the cultural fabric of an institution without the support of senior management. The support for this change culture must be both constant and genuine. The attainment of this institutional culture to partner everyday with change is neither a fad nor simply the fashionable thing to do. Change is clearly here to stay. It is crucial to have senior management fully supportive, because at some point it will become clear to the organization that thriving through change can only be accomplished when egos are left at the hitching post. Face-off!

Lesson 117

As long as an organization operates within traditional, vertical hierarchical relationships, where placing credit or blame is more important and more time consuming than meeting the needs of the market place, there is no possibility of achieving successful market synchronization.

The same can be said for day-to-day organizational decision-making. If all decision-making requires total consensus of all affected parties prior to possible implementation, the university will be stifled in all efforts of change management. If your institution is in those death grips of inertia, and if your institution is willing to relish in yesterday's successes, you will be doomed to a future of moats, mansions and the mass morass of mediocrity. You will undoubtedly find yourself both out-of-step and out-of-luck with your higher education competitors.

Lesson 118

Successful change management requires meeting the unique needs (mass customization) of our diverse set of customers when they want the service (market synchronization). The key to success is organizational flexibility and adaptability.

Effective change management provides the resources necessary to escape from lingering in the past, while still savoring the knowledge we have learned from our storied past. To advance in this world of change is often simply a question of will. Our success in the future rests with our understanding and our acceptance that we are not totally in control. We never were, but we thought we were! We can affect the outcome, but we do not control the outcome. Through the effective use of information, however, we now realize that some of our simplest processes can, and have been affected by a heretofore thought-to-be totally unrelated decision-making activities. Turnkey turbulence.

This knowledge is the key to our new beginning. Throughout every step of developing an institutional culture of continuous improvement at GMU, we have depended upon our people. They hold the key to our success, but we must provide them with the necessary support and direction. The front line group of staff ultimately responsible for the peak performance of each of our support services struggles mightily with the uncertainty associated with change. Within their group, however, there is leadership waiting to get the nod from you. It is all about getting used to surprises, regrouping, rethinking, and recasting the management of higher education! Advancing your institution through this stage of change and uncertainty will take a team of leaders from all levels and ranks within the organization.

The Art of Continuous Improvement

In the earlier chapters we discussed the role of the participants on the functional review team, the best practice search team, the RFP development team and the RFP evaluation team. The process of deciding upon the best shot at a best practice, is a grueling, rigorous activity. Continuity of team personnel is highly recommended throughout this process. However, if the support service is to continue to meet your needs after your delivery system decision, you must establish some type of group to keep the service on track.

Sometimes accomplishing this continuous improvement hinges upon selecting the right captain for your on-going review team. We have found that it is essential to identify, and then formalize the selection of a point person, whenever a function or an activity involves a number of different offices and/or individuals. The best practice lesson that we have learned is to select a person who demonstrated a "no fear" attitude toward failure combined with a "I won't let you down no matter what" guarantee. This kind of person usually takes great pride in accomplishing the task at hand, but generally give the credit to everyone else. These individuals also typically accept the blame when things do not go as well as planned. To some extent their reluctance to ever be fully satisfied with their efforts drives them toward continuous improvement in their quest for excellence. When searching for best practices, this is the kind of individual you want leading your team.

Selecting a point person to ensure support service effectiveness is one of the most important decisions you will make in finding blended management solutions. The search for this individual must be both title and employee-status blind. At GMU, we have selected contract employees to be the point person on some projects and we have selected staff individuals of fairly low rank to lead other projects. The point person must have a high level of service intimacy relative to the respective support service. As an organization, you will find out very quickly who talks the talk and who walks the walk when it comes to being a team player and leaving the egos outside.

Once the point person is selected, senior management must provide the necessary support, which always includes the setting of the team's rules of engagement. We have learned at GMU that we greatly improve our chances for continuous improvement success by eliminating any self-centered personal egos when we establish these ground rules for the group:

1. A control dominated supervisory mentality and an attitude that as a last resort one can always revert to title and power to get one's way is totally counter-productive and unacceptable.

2. A deference by those of lower title to those of higher title (or by contract employees to college or university staff) during team exercises, where the input of all members of the group is equally valued, greatly limits the potential accomplishments of the group.

3. The most likely reason for an outcome is not the performance of any particular person, but rather a perfect synchronization (or substantial malfunction) in the process.

The same group that planned and implemented the task, activity, function, or solution must engage in a timely critical post event review, and leave behind the necessary documentation (footprints) of their lessons learned and plans for service improvement for those that follow in the future.

We have also learned that not all tasks that involve multiple service departments lend themselves to the formation of teaming arrangements. Teams, as successful as they often may be, are not always the correct strategy to pursue in our quest for continuous improvement.

Team/Group Diversity

You cannot remind yourself often enough that you must avoid tunnel vision when establishing this continuous improvement sight adjusting team. A group consisting of the service manager, director of auxiliary enterprises, and a token student is not sufficient. Only through breadth and diversity of input do you have a change to objectively evaluate the effectiveness of your services.

For example, when our food service advisory group convenes to assess the food service (past efforts, current offerings and future plans) we can usually predict what each particular attendee will bring to the table. Our team is comprised of faculty, staff, students, and contract employees. Although you cannot always predict that a particular perspective will match up perfectly with each individual's day-to-day responsibilities, you can be pretty comfortable that some perspectives will not change very much.

The student representative typically will cite the issue of food quality and the variety of selection. Sometimes the underlying student complaint is really food presentation; sometimes it is the stoic environment of the facility, and then sometimes it is the personalities of the servers behind the counter. As long as the group listens, it has a chance to hear what is really on the minds of the students. The indispensable strength of the student input is familiarity with the consistency of the product. No one else eats the food every day of the year! Their weaknesses (understanding the operation, costs associated with enhanced service requirements, etc.) should be equally anticipated, but their participation is invaluable.

Likewise, the personnel from our food service contractor have traditionally brought to the table the highest standards and appreciation for quality of food and cleanliness of the facilities; an expert understanding of the food service operational requirements; and a variety of cost containment strategies that could reduce the cost to the university. Although this has varied over the years based upon the strengths of the individual corporate representative, the corporation typically demonstrates some weakness in the following areas: developing marketing strategies, projecting revenue growth for new concepts (generally defaulting to substitute sales rather than predicting new sales) and expanding aggressively into popular (but oftentimes costly) franchise products.

University staff has often brought to the team a sense of creativity and innovative approaches (late-night drive-through option, carryout and delivery, catering trucks around campus, etc.). On the other hand, the college or university staff (even the contract administrator) is often not fully aware of all the cost consequences associated with the proposed expansion of the number of points of food service delivery. Additionally, the college or university staff is usually not aware of the operational difficulties associated with attracting the type food service personnel necessary to provide the proposed innovative service.

To date we have always had the team chaired by a university staff member; however, we are considering rotating this chair to get a better view of the target of service excellence. We wonder whether a faculty or student leadership perspective give us the ultimate advantage toward a best practice.

The reason for sharing the strengths and weaknesses that parties bring to the year-long continuing search for best practices table as we evaluate our services is not to make judgments about our corporate partners, our own staff, or the students involved in the process. What is important about these teams is understanding what the players bring to the table. Other than sharing information and educating each other, we do not try to change the position of any of the individuals. By bringing together these different perspectives, we believe we have a much better opportunity to make the best decisions on continuous improvement. It is when your contract administrator stops listening and giving credence to what the others have to say about your services during these sessions that you are in the greatest danger.

---------------------- **Lesson 119** ----------------------

When debating organizational strategy it is not the conflict, or difference of opinions, that you must fear; it is the avoidance of these conflicts that will keep you from hitting your target of excellence.

Internal Isolationism = Institutional Ineffectiveness

Not all that long ago our staff within mail services had reached the point where they knew that the light at the end of the tunnel was most definitely a train coming the other direction. They felt that their backs were up against the wall, because the Commonwealth of Virginia was reducing the funding for GMU, and the university itself was trying to absorb the reductions as much as possible in the support services, thereby safeguarding the classroom. This strategy is not all that uncommon a philosophy for most institutions of higher education during times of funding reduction. The big problem for mail services was that although operations were not being fully funded, the university was still constructing new buildings on not only the Fairfax campus where mail services were housed, but also on the Prince William campus (15 miles to the southwest) and the Arlington campus (15 miles to the north). Rain, hail, snow, and sleet, timely mail delivery was our goal to meet.

This was a dilemma! The staff believed that they had a good view of their target of excellence, and they took their best shot. They established a mail stop number system for all delivery points throughout the campuses. They knew a similar system was working in many offices within the federal government, and they were sure that such a system could increase the efficiency of their unit here at GMU. To say this tactic was a disaster at GMU would be an understatement! Although they knew better, they took the proverbial shortcut! They listened to themselves, and only themselves! There had been no campus-wide dialogue of any consequence prior to implementation, and no assessment of the work transfer associated with this implementation. The fact that every departmental office would now be expected to learn everyone else's mail stop number; communicate this information to those parties mailing to GMU; revise all letterhead, business cards, etc., to now include mail stop numbers never became an issue of institutional dialogue. The discussion was not consciously avoided, it simply was not recognized. The downstream customer of this service change was simply not a voice that was ever heard.

The most condemning aspect of the decision was the lack of any communication to the field departments explaining the rationale and/or the benefits to be attained as a result of the change. There was no promise of more accurate or timely delivery. Even the logic of the mail stop numbers seemed to be at odds with the buildings and offices at GMU. We found out much later, much to our chagrin, that the mail stop numbering system was based on a military strategy board game, called Battleship.

"You may have to fight a battle more than once to win it."
—Margaret Thatcher

Although there was no single person to blame for this, a first reaction was to look for someone to hang from the closest tree. We were forced to relearn that every institution has multiple targets of excellence, and it is only by aligning those targets that one has any chance of being on target. Even a target as narrow as mail service operation efficiency is doomed to failure if the planners of the strategy are limited to only those directly responsible for the actual mail operation. We long ago had learned that without breadth of input at the takeoff, there would be great difficulties during the flight, as well as a high probability of a crash at the landing. Our frustration at the time of this particular crash came from our belief that we had already learned this lesson.

Lesson 120

An organizational change developed in isolation and/or a change that benefits solely the developing division must be given the light of day prior to implementation. Learning organizations recognize and appreciate the inter-relationships between divisions. Therefore, they understand and demand organizational breadth and input diversity.

Lesson 121

When too much pressure, stress, and time constraints are placed on staff, the natural tendency will be to revert to problematic quick fix solutions.

As we discussed earlier, it is incumbent upon an institution to know when it has approved such a quick-turnaround, time-sensitive solution. We have already agreed that such strategies must be:

- kept to a minimum;
- as unobtrusive on the campus community as possible; and
- totally reassessed in a timely fashion to modify and adjust as necessary to develop a broader, long term solution.

The mail stop number solution passed none of these tests. We went back to the drawing board and set up a review team comprised of representatives reflective of campus wide interests. The group recommended the improvements necessary, and the university subsequently outsourced the mail service. For the record, mail service has been dramatically improved over the past couple of years, and a revised, more user-friendly version of the original mail stop number system has been developed through this conversion. As is so often the case, it wasn't the idea that was the problem, it was the process of implementation.

Empowerment—Accountability

This original mail stop number debacle also gave us the opportunity to reassess our decentralized approach to operational management. We knew that although empowerment had been a key ingredient in our success of managing through change and being responsive to the needs of the market place, accountability was the foundation of our culture of change. Despite all the teaming, the partnering, the outsourcing, and the matrix managing strategies that we pursue, we knew that accountability must remain the one non-negotiable foundation for our future success. We are unwavering in our philosophy that authority and responsibility are not symmetrical. There may have been a day and a time where one could hope for authority commensurate with responsibility, but in today's learning organization we are generally responsible for much more than what we have direct authority to control. There is direct authority and accountability, and as an organization we attempt to be very clear about where that accountability rests. Similarly, there is shared responsibility and we attempt to ensure that our affected staff associates understand where they hold some responsibility for the success of activities outside their official organization.

Lesson 122

If we do not reinforce the concept of personal as well as group responsibility as we build a culture of empowerment, we will lose accountability. No organization should be willing to walk down the path of empowerment without the organizational understanding of all affected parties that this is a two-way street. Successful empowerment equates to decentralized accountability.

Tools for Success

We have discovered over the years that the natural tendency of an organization will always be to retreat to its respective comfort zones of operation, especially when the heat from supervisory personnel is being turned up a little higher. With that realization, it is essential that you provide staff with the best possible shot selection for success when looking to implement change management. We have developed three tools that help us retain adaptability and keep us advancing forward in our pursuit of improvement.

Keys to Change Management

- Swat Culture
- Venture Capital

- Surge Space

First, we put together carefully selected swat teams wherever possible. At GMU, this phrase came from former president, George W. Johnson, who during his 17-year tenure would typically give assignments to staff by asking them to "swat something up" for him. It just seemed to make sense for us to put together swat teams to swat up recommendations to cross-organizational issues.

Organization units understand the institutional benefits derived from these efforts, and they therefore pitch-in to keep day-to-day operations running efficiently when a member of their office is detailed to a swat assignment. The critical prerequisites to a swat team assignment includes complexity of issue, inter-service consequences, institutional importance and length (short!) of assignment. The results of swat team efforts are always widely disseminated throughout the campus.

Venture capital is our second tool that helps us maintain agility. Venture capital is allocated exclusively to support non-recurring, one-time opportunities. The actual release of the funds is linked to the timing of the opportunity investment. The recipient of these funds has no assurance or expectation of continuation of any specific level of funding. It is either given to cover a one-time cost or to kick start an initiative with self-sustaining future year potential. It is only through our institutional discipline to annually reallocate two percent of our resources from within the base that we are able to continue venture capital funding.

As much as being young and lean has been an advantage for GMU, those same attributes can sometimes cause problems. Because we are young, we simply do not have the resources of the older, more established universities of similar size and complexity. However, despite the lack of funding comparable to more established institutions of similar size and complexity, GMU selectively captures two percent of the operating budget every year and reallocates these funds to high priority initiatives. These upcoming-year priorities are usually a combination of addressing prior-year deficiencies, as well as new initiatives. As difficult as it has been, the university always budgets a venture capital reserve.

The third tool is creating surge space. We have been much less successful in creating surge space to support those investments requiring space, but we have developed an institutional culture that will readily negotiate an off-campus lease agreement if an opportunity arises that requires an allocation of space. Adaptability usually requires the use of some combination of these tools. The easiest strategy for us to initiate has been the concept of swat teams. Staff is on stand-by to be called into active duty as a swat team member. It's an exciting assignment! The importance of swat teams, surge space, and venture capital cannot be overstated. We believe these investments are inseparable with the culture of change management, agility, and adaptability. Organizational agility will not be created overnight, and you must be willing to make an institutional commitment of time and effort required to be successful in attaining this objective.

Lesson 123

You must be willing to invest in change for change to be a good investment for you. There is no free lunch!

Timeliness is critical if we are to take advantage of an opportunity that appears to be central to the mission of the institution. This ability to maneuver quickly is not the typical mindset of a public institution. It is much more common for colleges and universities to allocate every available dollar to an existing operation; allocate every square foot of space to a department; deliberate endlessly through committee meetings over every complex dilemma; and thereby lose any capacity to respond to a time sensitive opportunity. What is most distressing about these common institutional attributes is that they tend to be true, no matter how critical the potential outcome or how fleeting the opportunity.

Lesson 124

The rationale behind this "time is of an essence" philosophy is that agility and adaptability require an organizational mentality that is committed to making the decisions and taking the action when they are needed.

If nothing else, we must be totally committed to attaining and retaining this elusive quality of institutional agility. However, heed these words of caution as you attempt to become a more agile institution: First, a laissez faire mentality with no lines of authority and accountability is not the blueprint for developing institutional agility. Second, do not be fooled by slick window dressing associated with internal restructuring efforts. The natural tendency of a university to revert to its own comfort zone is not limited exclusively to units returning to old, safe organizational hierarchies. There will also be a natural tendency to build and establish new bureaucracies under the guise of change. You must be sensitive to, and protect against, this potentiality. Bureaucracies, whether new or old, tend to build walls and other forms of protection that are debilitating to your efforts for continuous improvement.

Lesson 125

Do not be fooled by organizational changes that simply create new organizational structures without achieving organizational flexibility, adaptability, and agility.

Conclusion

The journey for best practices will include many unforeseen detours and retraced steps. We must remember that the learning occurs along the trail, not in arriving at the summit. The learning occurs when we are not certain which fork in the road to take, and when we have no map or footsteps to follow. This search for excellence is a test of courage if it is nothing else. The journey requires shared leadership, commitment, and capacity.

Throughout these chapters, we have emphasized the importance of each of these characteristics, and we have advised you that the best way to accomplish this task of finding a best practice is to dedicate yourself to the development of a learning organization. By blending a shared organizational mission with both a structure of internal adaptability and a commitment to understanding, guiding, and directing a diverse set of associates, you create your best chance to achieve your best practice objectives.

Organizational Strengths: Building by Blending

We all must invest in the resources necessary to take us to the new millenium. Blended management combines the best and brightest thinkers from within your organization with those from outside corporations. When these best and brightest are guided by the high-five approach to management, we are in the best possible position for achieving our exceptional performance. When motivated by a clear and concise understanding of the mission, we have a chance to mold our team together. We must continue our blending, because today's internal and external factors are never the same as yesterday's, and will look nothing like those of the future. The management of change, or should we say, the capacity to embrace change, is what separates the wheat from the chaff. We can survive, and even thrive, during chaos, confusion and constant change. But to flourish during these times, we must first and foremost be true to ourselves. The only way to stay a step ahead of the competition is to understand ourselves. We must be able to answer why we are what we are, before we can engage in any meaningful dialogue about our search for best practices. This is our epiphany!

Choice—Chance—Change

As leaders of our organizations, we must enlist and then engage the staff in embracing the concept of continuous change. It is our future!

No matter how successful our college or university, or how happy our employees seem to be, we must make it an enjoyable place to be. We cannot fool anyone if we are not ourselves—fulfilled! Finding best practices must be a priority. We must build our team and attack the frontier of the unknown with passion and purpose.

It is no coincidence that "change" and "chance" are spelled so similarly. The risk associated with embracing change is irrefutable, but we really have no choice. We must learn to embrace change, because it provides our only chance to flourish during times of change.

There is no reason for fear or reluctance. We shall enjoy the moment; celebrate each success; learn from every misstep; and remember the most important lesson of all:

> *"To enjoy the things we ought to enjoy . . . has the greatest bearing on excellence of character."*
>
> —Aristotle